THE BIRTH
OF THE
LUFTWAFFE

HANFRIED SCHLIEPHAKE

LONDON

IAN ALLAN

First published 1971

For my wife

SBN 7110 0206 1

*Published by Ian Allan Ltd, Shepperton, Surrey and printed in the
United Kingdom by Morrison and Gibb Ltd, London and Edinburgh*

Contents

Foreword

by ALFRED PRICE

As ANY PROPAGANDIST, or advertising man, will tell you, if a statement is repeated often enough it will usually come to be accepted as fact. No body of men was ever the subject of a greater or a more sustained barrage of false propaganda than the *Luftwaffe* between 1933 and 1945, much of it coming from the Germans themselves. But, behind the propaganda facade, accurate and detailed official records were being kept. By making available this painstakingly accurate account of the German Air Force between the wars, based on official records made at the time, Hanfried Schliephake is performing a great service to historians. Such a book has been long overdue.

Hanfried Schliephake flew with the *Luftwaffe* in the Second World War, and he is again as a flying officer in that force. He is, therefore, professionally well qualified to sift through and evaluate the mass of research material he had gathered for this work. The outcome is a highly detailed account which gives us an intimate view of the building of the *Luftwaffe*. And as might be expected in such a work, some old and well-worn myths are crushed. In particular, there is a new insight into the cancellation of the Dornier 19 and the Junkers 89—both of them four-engined heavy bombers—while in the flight test stage; the often quoted view, that this marked the end of any interest by the *Luftwaffe* high command in strategic bombing, is firmly quashed.

The text of this work is sufficiently comprehensive and revealing to stand on its own. But Schliephake does not stop there. With it he has included a unique selection of photography from his own vast collection. Of particular fascination are the shots taken at the secret training base at Lipezk deep in Russia, as well as those of such long-forgotten German military aircraft as the Rohrbach Roland and the Dornier P.

With this combination of text and photographs, Hanfried Schliephake has produced an important reference work. It is one which, in my opinion, no serious student of the *Luftwaffe* can afford not to have on his bookshelf.

Introduction

IN THIS BOOK I have tried to give a brief and chronological account of the history of the German *Luftwaffe* in the period between the two Great Wars in Europe, to show how it was built up and how it acquitted itself. Brief and incomplete as this account inevitably is, I hope that it may help to dispel the legends that have grown up and persisted through the years, such as the one put out by the propagandists of the Third Reich to the effect that the *Luftwaffe* was conjured into existence and launched on a meteoric career when the Nazis seized power on January 30, 1933, whereas in fact its revival was based on a solid foundation that had been very carefully laid by the *Reichswehr* authorities in the preceding years of preparation. And in this connection, the good relationship established with the 'Red Army' in Russia was of vital significance. The air-base at Lipezk, for instance, provided an ideal substitute for the lack of training facilities at home. Lipezk enabled tactical and technical experience to be gained, and a cadre of trained personnel to be built up. The work done there by the officers of the *Reichswehr* and the staff of the testing station deserves recognition.

Another widespread but equally mistaken myth is that the development of a long-range bomber in line with the Douhet philosophy was immediately abandoned when the Chief of the Air Staff General Wever died, on June 3, 1936. At no time did the General Staff of the *Luftwaffe* reject the long-range bomber as a strike aircraft. The material for this account of the build-up of German air power came from a number of sources, first and foremost from the documentary archives of the Institute of Military History[1] at Freiburg, and especially the publications of Karl-Heinz Völker to whom I owe a particular debt of gratitude also for permission to use photographs taken at Lipezk at the time when it was a German air-base. Other material was derived from earlier works published by General der Flieger a.D. Helm Speidel, and supplied by former members of testing station staff, not least among them Willy Radinger who helped me greatly with the loan of documents and photographs from his own collection. I am also indebted to the many others who provided me with photographs from their archives, or collections, especially Hans Redemann (Editor of the 'Flug-Revue+flugwelt international'), Fritz Trenkle, Botho v. Römer, Wolfgang Wagner (Publisher of the 'deutscher aerokurier') and Walter Zuerl (Publisher of the 'Der Flieger'), also Deutsche Lufthansa AG

[1] *Militärgeschichtliches Forschungsamt.*

(Photo service) and the firms of Dornier GmbH, Heinkel now Vereinigte
Flugtechnische Werke GmbH (VFW), and Messerschmitt now Messerschmitt-
Bölkow-Blohm GmbH (MBB). Some of the pictures reproduced in the
book derive from calendars, recruiting posters and other material published by
the *Wehrmacht*, while others are reproductions of snapshots taken by former
members of the *Luftwaffe* and kindly put at my disposal by them or their
families, to all of whom I express my gratitude for their co-operation.

HANFRIED SCHLIEPHAKE

Königsbrunn/Augsburg.

CHAPTER ONE

Work Behind the Scenes

I will go on fighting for Germany's right to equality of status with all the passion and persistence for which we old national socialists are noted, until I know the safety of the German nation is assured.

Hermann Goering

THUS HERMANN GOERING, on January 30, 1933, announced the building up of the German air force. And on July 13, 1940, in a summary of the situation on the West front delivered at a meeting of the *Reichstag*, Hitler had this to say about Goering's achievements:

> 'Throughout the reconstruction of the German armed forces Goering has been the creator of the German air force. History knows only very few instances of anyone, in the course of a single life, creating a military instrument from scratch and developing it into the most powerful force of its kind in existence.'

Among the eulogies heaped on Goering at the height of his career was a comparison with Scharnhorst whose iron will and boundless energy he was said to share. But was there any truth in this label of 'Scharnhorst of the German air force', in the claim that Goering conjured up the German air force out of a void as if it had been a phoenix rising from the ashes? The answer history gives is a clear 'no'.

The new German air force in fact arose out of years of planning and practical work done by the aeronautical branches of the military and naval staffs in the Reich Ministry of Defence. When the camouflage was discarded, in 1935, and the revived air force was allowed to appear on the world scene in the full light of day, the myth about its having been created out of nothing was so convincingly staged that not only the world press but even the secret services in other countries fell for it. As a result of the 'psychological warfare' based on the complete success of this piece of deception, the extent and striking power of the German air force came to be grossly exaggerated, with widespread and dire consequences in the months preceding the outbreak of the Second World War.

The Treaty of Versailles, which came into force on January 10, 1920, prohibited Germany *inter alia* from adding air formations to her residual land and sea defence forces. Three months later, on April 9, 1920, the army Chief-of-Staff, General von Seeckt, at the request of the Ambassadors' Conference then in session in Paris, ordered the disbanding of the few remaining air formations.

The applications made by the German government for permission to retain eight air stations and a single squadron of aircraft in operation was rejected by the Ambassadors' Conference in spite of the fact that the request had been made not for military reasons but for reasons of internal security, i.e. for the maintenance of law and order. Even the seven police air patrol squadrons, established in 1919 by the governments of the individual *Länder* to assist in the work of the police forces, were disbanded in 1920. The final disbanding of the German flying corps was ordered by the head of army command in an order of the day drafted by Captain (later General) Wilberg of the air staff and dated May 6, 1920. It reads, in part, as follows:

'**Disbandment of the flying corps.** As from May 8, 1920, a young branch of the armed forces, which has served with bravery in action and earned fame in the course of its relatively short history, will lay down arms in silence and with pride. On this day, the German Flying Corps fulfils the demand laid down in the Peace Treaty for the complete disbanding of all its formations and establishments.'

There follows a brief account of the history and organisation of the Corps and of its wartime achievements. The closing words read:

'We shall not abandon the hope of one day seeing the Flying Corps come to life again. The fame of the Flying Corps engraved in the history of the German armed forces will never fade. It is not dead, its spirit lives on!
    Charged with the carrying out of this order.'
                                          (signed) v Seeckt

Many of the airmen in the service derived consolation and hope from this wording, and it is therefore understandable that efforts were made to conceal air force equipment instead of surrendering it. These efforts could not of course be kept secret, with the result that the Army Command in January 1921 imposed heavy penalties for any action contravening the terms of the disbanding order, since such action could have serious consequences for the German people as a whole.

Even defence ministry circles clung to the hope that military aviation might eventually be reinstated, and so attempts were made to maintain a hidden reserve of trained pilots, air-crew and ground staff. These efforts succeeded in the case of some 120 former military pilots and 20 former naval air arm pilots who remained in the armed forces after 1920. The problem of retaining air force NCOs and ground personnel proved very much more difficult.

Some former military pilots succeeded in getting service appointments abroad, others transferred to civil aviation, but the majority found their way into civilian life. The terms of the Versailles Treaty hit the German aircraft industry particularly hard. Article 201 prohibited Germany for a period of six months from the date on which it came into force, from 'manufacturing or importing any aircraft or component thereof, as also any aircraft engine or part thereof, throughout the whole of German territory'. This prohibition and embargo remained in force after the London Ultimatum, and it was not until a year after that, that Germany was allowed to build aircraft, and then only within the limits specified in a set of definitions laid down by the Ambassadors' Conference and issued on April 14, 1922. These definitions were designed specifically to preclude the development of military aircraft by imposing performance limits of 110mph speed, 170 miles range, $2\frac{1}{2}$ hours flying time, 16,000 feet ceiling, and a very light service load. Observance of the limitations was to be enforced by an Allied Commission which was appointed with the title of Interallied-Military-Control-Commission (IMKK). As far as civil aviation was concerned, these limitations were superseded by the terms of the Aviation Convention signed in Paris in May 1926.

Long before this time, the last trace of a German air force had ceased to exist, and the situation was in complete accord with the provisions of the Treaty of Versailles. And then a surprising thing happened. On April 16, 1922, the German and Soviet delegations concluded a separate treaty at Rapallo, without awaiting the outcome of the International World Economic Conference held at Genoa to which Germany and the Soviet Union were admitted for the first time with equal rights. Prior to this, Germany and the Soviet Union had concluded a Trade Agreement on May 6, 1921, as a result of which discussions were started on economic and technical aspects of the military defence situation which led ultimately to direct contact between the Russian negotiator Radek and General von Seeckt. These military discussions undoubtedly contributed to the conclusion of the Treaty of Rapallo, which General von Seeckt welcomed most keenly since he saw in it a stepping stone to the realisation of his ideas on a future German defence policy. The treaty provided for the mutual renunciation of reparations, expansion of trade relations and the immediate resumption of diplomatic relations. While it cost Germany the confidence of the West, the Rapallo treaty did lay the foundation for years of collaboration between the *Reichswehr* and the Red Army which enabled Germany to slip the shackles imposed on her freedom of action in defence matters, for instance by participating in the development and testing of weapons denied to Germany by the Versailles Treaty.

Before this collaboration could become effective, prolonged and difficult negotiations had to be conducted with the Soviet Union, for which purpose a commission was set up consisting of members of the camouflaged air staffs of the military and naval departments of the German ministry of defence and sent to Moscow, under assumed names, after being officially posted as sick. After completion of their mission, the 'Moscow Detachment', led by a Herr von der Lieth, remained in Moscow as a liaison unit. The name 'Herr von der Lieth' in fact concealed the identity of a retired Colonel von der Lieth-Thomsen, who had been Chief of Air Staff under the Air Force C-in-C in the First World War.

At that time, the *Reichswehr* authorities were striving to find ways and means to provide air support for the ground forces in view of the constant danger of conflict with Poland and of the 1923 crisis in the Ruhr. The German government was even toying with the idea of military resistance to the threatened French occupation of the Ruhr. However, Captain Wilberg, of whom mention has already been made and who was official rapporteur to the camouflaged aviation department of the ministry of defence, was not in a position to make any existing reserves of aircraft available for this purpose. He therefore decided, with the backing of the government, to order 100 fighter aircraft from the Dutch firm of Fokker, to be financed out of the Ruhr Fund. In the event, delivery was delayed beyond the critical date, and in any case the government decided against putting up any military resistance in the Ruhr. It then looked as if procuring the Fokker fighters had been a military blunder. When the negotiations with the Russians were successfully concluded, however, there was an immediate need for 50 Fokker Type D XIII fighters for the tactical training of fighter pilots and cadets at the military flying school established at Lipezk in Russia (see Appendix A).

From the final minutes of the Russo-German conference, dated April 15, 1925, it appears that an arrangement was reached between Lieth then in charge of the 'Moscow Detachment' and the Russian air force chief, Baranov, to the effect that these aircraft were to be shipped to Russia through the port of Leningrad. These minutes also contain preliminary details relating to the establishment and running of the projected flying school. Air-to-ground firing practice, for instance, was to be carried out over suitable territory to be allocated to the school.

The first training course at Lipezk was started in the early summer of 1925, intended primarily as an exercise in Russo-German collaboration. The first regular course was started in the same year after the arrival of the 50 Fokker D XIII fighter aircraft which had left the port of Stettin on board the *Edmund Hugo Stinnes 4* on May 28, 1925. The remainder of the aircraft originally ordered from Fokker, consisting of D VIIs and D XIs, were sold to the air forces of other countries between 1923 and 1925. A small number of D VIIs was delivered to Lipezk at a later date.

In 1923, quite independently of the Fokker procurement, the then Major Student got in touch with Ernst Heinkel at Warnemünde and gave him, under the seal of the strictest secrecy, an order to build a land biplane designed to be used as a short-range reconnaissance aircraft. After the definition came into force, Ernst Heinkel had continued to concern himself with aircraft design and construction, on a modest scale. Referring to the order placed with him by Student, Heinkel said at a later date, 'With the development of the first aircraft destined for service with the armed forces of the Reich, the HD 17, an extremely risky game of hide-and-seek with the Allied Control Commission began, and I am bound to admit that it was a game that was bound to appeal strongly to a man who was given to taking risks.' And it is true to say that this sentiment was echoed by the many other plane-makers in the German aircraft industry who, in order not to fall behind other countries in technical ability and experience, resumed building aircraft, some at home and others abroad so as to avoid breaking the enforced limitations. Heinkel, who had only one workshop hangar, hired another one in which he built what he called his pet prototypes. The members of the Allied Control Commission never saw this hangar otherwise than swept and garnished. Hours before they arrived on the scene, every single aircraft component and item of equipment had been loaded on lorries and parked in concealed spots on the heath or between the sand-dunes, to reappear only when the coast was clear.

The Heinkel aircraft developed and built in the years 1923 and 1924 for the *Reichswehr* were the HD 17 and HD 21. Only a small number of HD 17s was built and they were used along with HD 21s at Lipezk. The naval division of the Reich Defence Ministry also placed an order with the Heinkel works at Warnemünde for their first 10 aircraft so as to have at least a few naval fighters available; they were of Type S1/He 1, a developed version of the Hansa Brandenburg W 29 dating from 1918. The order was conveyed through an uncommitted go-between and the purchase money remitted by the government through special channels. The components were designed and built at Warnemünde and subsequently assembled and tested in Sweden. The engines were Rolls-Royce Eagle IXs, since engines of German manufacture were not available at that time. The aircraft were packed in huge packing-cases and warehoused in bond at Stockholm harbour by the firm owned by the former naval Commander Bücker.

In addition, Commander Ritter succeeded in buying up six wartime aircraft of the Friedrichshafen FF 49 type before they could be seized for reparations delivery abroad. The price paid for these aircraft, at the end of the period of the inflation, was 1,000 Marks in the new stabilized currency (£100) for each machine including the engine. The last of these aircraft remained in operation up to 1934, for towing floats used in anti-speedboat exercises. They were

maintained and serviced by Aero-Lloyd[1] and used for general military purposes such as AA gunnery practice, camouflage exercises, target-towing and
personnel training. They were based at Kiel-Holtenau and Norderney.

With great difficulty, permission was obtained for airmen still on the naval
strength, from 1924 onwards, to take a refresher flying course run by the firm
of Aerosport GmbH (Direktor Bachmann) at Warnemünde and to be trained
as fully operational pilots. This training had to be handled with the greatest
care because the Allies were trying to get hold of the names of all pilots trained
in Germany. Furthermore, under the terms of the Paris Aviation Convention,
only a very strictly limited number of service personnel were allowed to receive
flying instruction and to serve as airmen in the armed forces. The number was
limited to six, and they were only allowed to receive 'sport' type flying instruction. For this reason, the camouflaged Aviation Inspectorate (In 1) in the
personnel department of the Reich ministry of defence issued an instruction to
the effect that a certain number of officer cadets were to be given flying
instruction prior to call-up. This applied to approximately 40 cadets per
annum. Only in this way was it possible to build up a basic reserve of personnel
in readiness for the eventual resuscitation of the air force. Rearmament in the
air became an integral part of general rearmament, providing for a step-by-step
build-up of fighter, reconnaissance and courier squadrons.

In the beginning, the training facilities available in Germany were limited to
the few existing civil flying schools[2] located mainly in Brunswick and at
Schleissheim near Munich. They had to be utilized for military purposes
without this being apparent to the outside observer. All the pupils received
the same basic training up to B2 pilot's licence standard. The annual reliability
tests were also conducted at these schools. In this way the total number of
trained flying personnel grew steadily. These officers of the army and navy
were also enabled to attend a number of aeronautical meetings, to enter for
gliding competitions in the Rhön district, and to take part in German and other
European air races.

But the final stages of their training, i.e. for service in a particular type of
military aircraft, could only be carried out abroad. For this purpose the German
flying school at Lipezk, located about 250 miles SSW of Moscow, constituted
the main Reichswehr base on Russian soil. Here the young cadets could be
trained, on a modest scale, and could acquire aeronautical and technical experience. The machines turned out by the German aircraft industry could be fitted
with military equipment and put through tactical and technical trials. In spite
of the greatest efforts at concealment, it was not feasible to carry out trials of
this nature from the Reichswehr aerodrome at Rechlin am Müritzsee which

[1] Later: Severa.
[2] 'Sportflug GmbH' with 10 flying schools at: Königsberg, Stettin, Staaken, Warnemünde, Schkeuditz, Böblingen, Hanover, Würzburg.

was camouflaged to resemble an industrial aircraft testing station. Lipezk thus had a dual function, as a military flying school and also as a testing station for military aircraft.

The first commandant at Lipezk, from 1924 to 1930, was the former Major a. D. Stahr after whom, for reasons of secrecy, the flying school was named. During the summer months the total staff (military and civilian) numbered, on average, 200 of whom about 50 were engaged in running the military training courses. After 1930, owing to an increase in the number of technical trials conducted there, the staff was increased to 300. The German staff was interspersed at all times with Russian personnel, partly auxiliaries and partly pupil-technicians.

The commandant of the school had under his command:

the staff group equipped with a Junkers F 13 and A 20 as well as three test aircraft which were mainly used for courier and transport purposes (the F 13 was subsequently replaced by a W 33);

the observer squadron equipped with two Heinkel HD 17s;

the fighter squadron equipped with 18 Fokker D XIIIs;

the observer training course equipped with four Heinkel HD 17s;

the fighter training course equipped with 16 Fokker D XIIIs, two Heinkel HD 17s, two Albatros L 69s, one Fokker D VII, and one Heinkel HD 21.

The commandant also had under him a junior flying school equipped with four trainers, a test group, workshops, and depot.

The annual budget for meeting the cost of running the Lipezk establishment was 2 million Marks (£200,000). The layout comprised two runways with a number of hangars and workshop buildings, and an up-to-date engine test-bed, also administration and living accommodation blocks and a fully equipped modern hospital building. The entire complex was expertly camouflaged to resemble the 4th Eskadrille of a Russian air force unit, with the help of the constant presence of a few obsolete Russian reconnaissance aircraft.

The flying instruction had to be completely revised to comply with changing conditions and needs, since the principles on which training during the war had been based were now completely out-of-date and useless. New principles had to be worked out empirically on which to base, progressively, a new training schedule. At Lipezk this work of evolving a new system of training was carried out by instructors and pupils jointly, covering all aspects—flying, tactics, organisation and technology; here the mental background for a future German air force was forged in the fire of day-to-day flying practice and the work this entailed.

The first job was to train up instructor personnel and to hold refresher courses for wartime pilots. The first intake of young Reichswehr officers at Lipezk arrived in 1926, and a year later training began of the Jungmärker, as they were called. The trained pilots were known as Altmärker.

The fighter pilot training courses were held in the summer months and lasted 20–22 weeks. In the winter months, when there were no flying pupils at Lipezk, the instructors were engaged in tactical and formation flying exercises. Training was carried out in accordance with the newly-evolved principles. Tactical flying was taught in a gradual progression from solo flying, through delta to close formation flying, and finally air combat exercises culminating in a mock air battle between two squadrons of nine aircraft a side. The poor climbing performance of the then available aircraft, coupled with the lack of oxygen apparatus in the late 1920s made it necessary to restrict fighter pilot training to low level attack exercises. The aircraft were additionally equipped with bomb release gear and used as fighter-bomber trainers.

Between 1925 and 1933 about 120 officers completed their training as fighter pilots and were capable, after a brief period of retraining, of handling any modern type of aircraft. The navigation course at Lipezk took a year preceded by a six months preliminary course in Berlin concerned mainly with tactical theory and practical WT operation. The next six months, spent at Lipezk itself, were devoted to training in the air on navigation, WT operation and gunnery practice, and sometimes in bomb-aiming.

On a training site near Voronesh tactical flying exercises were carried out in conjunction with Russian artillery and ground forces, under the most primitive, field type conditions. In particular, artillery guidance and ranging were practised, and new ranging methods worked out and tested. Between 1928 and 1930 about 100 officers were trained as artillery observers.

Military aircraft and equipment underwent the most rigorous performance testing for military purposes by specialist engineers under the guidance of army ordnance officers. This procedure was extended to include all instruments and items of equipment used on military aircraft, such as armament, bombs, aiming devices and reflex sights, and was carried out with the meticulous thoroughness for which German craftsmen are noted. The Russians showed great interest in these tests, and groups of Russian air force officers and technicians watched the procedures with close attention. Even prominent officials from the Zagi air armament testing station used to make a practice of being present, along with technical personnel, during the test runs in the early 1930s. At that time the Russians themselves had nothing to show which would have justified a mutual exchange of technical knowledge and experience. For the rest, there was relatively little in the way of tactical co-operation in the matter of training at Lipezk in those days.

Joint exercises with a Russian formation took place for the first time in 1932, from which useful experience and some progress in connection with modes of attack used against bombers operating in daylight were gained. A projected joint fighter exercise intended to enable the respective air combat tactics to be compared with each other was eventually abandoned after having been repeatedly called off by the Russians. An air show staged by the Russians near Moscow did not produce anything new either.

The highlight of each testing session used to be an exhibition and a demonstration of all available aeronautical equipment for the benefit of a Russian commission. On these occasions not only was the technical equipment laid open to inspection but Red air force pilots, who in this case were undoubtedly experienced test pilots, were given an opportunity to fly the German machines. Thus as far back as 1931 the Russians received detailed insight into all German tested aircraft and their military equipment. When the build-up of the new Air Force was started in 1933, these aircraft were available as standard models ready for expanded series production.

The most difficult and at the same time most intriguing job with which the Reich Defence Ministry had been faced was undoubtedly how to keep the whole organisation secret. To this end, for example, all frontier traffic, in both directions, was handled by two institutions camouflaged as registered trading companies. Items of military equipment which could not be effectively concealed or camouflaged, such as new types of bomb, were smuggled across the Baltic, at night or in foggy weather, by Reichswehr officers in small sailing vessels, often at the risk of their lives. Aircraft were flown at high altitudes, in a single hop, to one of the border countries, generally at night. The coffins containing the bodies of airmen who lost their lives at Lipezk had to be crated and declared as machine parts, and smuggled out of the harbour at Stettin with the connivance of customs officials who had been let into the secret.[1] After completion of their training, the airmen travelled as passengers on board Russian ships sailing from Leningrad across the Baltic, to land unnoticed by climbing over the dykes of the North Sea/Baltic canal at night. The organisation even succeeded in getting the Napier Lion engines used on the Fokker D XIII and the Heinkel HD 17 to the makers' works in England, for repair, and then back to the Russian base, without the deception being discovered.

Apart from those already mentioned, no other types of training aircraft were delivered to Lipezk for instruction purposes, although the school did ask for replacement of the obsolescent Fokker D XIIIs and Heinkel HD 17s by more up-to-date types including two Junkers K 47s equipped with dual controls for practice in combat tactics against two-seater fighters. The Junkers K 47 and the Focke-Wulf Fw 39 short-range reconnaissance aircraft were eliminated from the then current Reichswehr equipment programme owing to the results of the trials carried out in the summer of 1931. There were, however, still some thirty Fokker D XIIIs, four Heinkel HD 17s and two Fokker D VIIs

[1] Three fatal accidents happened between 1924 and 1933.

available for fighter training purposes until the school was abandoned (see Appendix B).

In response to invitations to tender issued by the aviation section of the Army Ordnance Office in 1929[1] for the designing of a short-range reconnaissance, a long-range reconnaissance, a fighter and a bomber aircraft, the German aircraft industry produced, one after another, in the years immediately following a number of new aircraft models for so-called front-line testing at Lipezk. In the course of 1931, two Arado Ar 64s and a Heinkel HD 38 underwent this testing procedure, and in both cases created a favourable impression, particularly in comparative tests with the Fokker D XIII. The types of Heinkel short- and long-range reconnaissance aircraft tested at Lipezk were the He 46 and He 45. Both were taken in hand by the ex-Eng-Col. Schwenke and demonstrated by him to the Russians. During the ferrying of the Heinkel He 46, Schwenke was compelled by an engine fault to make a forced landing near Vitebsk.[2]

The bombers tested at Lipezk were the Dornier Do P, and later on the Dornier Do 11 and the Rohrbach Roland. The Roland was a standard type as used by the Lufthansa equipped with several MG turrets to enable experience to be gained with defensive armament. One particularly noteworthy fact is that this modification was carried out at the Rohrbach works in Germany without the ubiquitous Control Commission getting wind of it. Once, when the Control Commission carried out a surprise tour of inspection at the works, it was impossible to conceal the aircraft in which the MG armament had already been installed in extra-long engine pods. The simple but ingenious ruse was adopted, on the spur of the moment, of placing the machine in the middle of the hangar and cluttering it up with dust-covers, staging, ladders and other bits of workshop equipment so that it looked like a heap of unwanted stuff. The inspectors repeatedly went past it without an inkling of what was hidden under it.

Before the end of May 1933, the Dornier Do P was test-flown at Lipezk; this aircraft, like the Rohrbach Roland was later replaced by the Dornier Do 11 designed on the basis of the results of the testing at Lipezk. At this time, the

---

[1] First developments (Hptm Student period), Heinkel HD 41, so-called 'Erkunigros' (*Erkundungsflugzeug für mittlere Höhen und größte Entfernungen, gleichzeitig mittlerer Bomber*), reconnaisance plane for medium altitudes and long-range as well as medium size bomber.

Messerschmitt M 22, so-called 'Najaku' (*Nachtjagd und Erkundungsflugzeug*), night-fighter and reconnaissance aircraft.

Albatros L 84 and Arado SD 1, so-called 'Heitag' (*Heimatjagdeinsitzer*), fighter aircraft.

Albatros L 76/77 later L 78, so-called 'Erkudista' (*Erkundungsflugzeug für die Divisions-nahaufklärungsstaffeln*), tactical reconnaissance aircraft.

[2] Ferry-routes: From Rechlin or Travemünde to Lipezk via East Prussia, Lithuania and Latvia. The air corridor for approaching Russia was near the town Welikje-Luki.

Russians were showing extremely keen interest in bomber development and letting it be understood that they wished the Reichswehr authorities, from then on, to train night-flying bomber formations on a large scale in Russia. The reason for this request may well have been the assumption that the Reichswehr had developed bombers in accordance with the Douhet Theory which it was intended to keep secret from them.

Further aircraft which underwent front-line testing in 1932 and 1933 were the prototype Heinkel He 51, the Arado Ar 65 and, finally, the Junkers W 34, Heinkel HD 59 and Dornier Do 11, all listed in the Service Schedule for the period 1929–1933.

As Germany progressively regained freedom of action, the first step taken, in 1930, was to transfer the observer training unit back to Germany. It then became possible to step up pilot training in Germany as well, for which the commercial flying school (DVS) at Brunswick and, for initial training, the DVS at Schleissheim near Munich could be made available. Refresher courses were laid on at the v Greim flying club school at Würzburg. Basic fighter training continued at Lipezk.

Before Hitler's seizure of power, the Reich Defence Ministry already intended to abandon the establishment at Lipezk. Later on Hitler ordered the liquidation of all military links with Russia, and in the autumn of 1933 an officer of the General Staff was sent to Russia to supervise the disbanding of the Lipezk base. This was at the conclusion of the summer session of fighter training and technical testing programmes, and flying then came to an end, with the aircraft standing ready to fly back to Germany. There was tension in the air as negotiations started for the disbanding and handing-over. The Russian negotiator clearly had his eye not only on the ground equipment, hangars, workshops and so on, but also on all the aircraft which had just gone through their trials, these being aircraft developed since 1931 and destined to form the backbone of German rearmament in the air. The compromise finally reached at the highest level was to the effect that Germany could transfer all movable equipment including aircraft to Germany, while the Russians received, in compensation, the aerodrome together with all buildings and equipment and, in addition, the aircraft which had been used for instruction purposes including thirty Fokker D XIIIs. These latter aircraft were in any case in no condition to withstand the flight to Germany.

By September 1933, the German air base at Lipezk had ceased to exist. The front-line aircraft and armament tested at Lipezk then stood ready, as standard types, to form the basis already worked out to the last detail for large-scale series production by the German aircraft industry. The personnel trained at Lipezk numbered 450, mostly officers, and a corresponding number of highly qualified ground staff, ready to provide a core of experts and instructors for a future full-scale Air Force. These men had, in the time spent at Lipezk, outlived the trauma of defeat in the First World War, and had regained confidence and the fighting spirit of which General v Seeckt had spoken in May 1920 in his order to disband the old air force. Lipezk had also played a key role in enabling the Reich Defence Ministry to build up a highly qualified group of air ordnance experts on which the Reich Air Ministry could draw to establish the General Staff of the new *Luftwaffe*.

CHAPTER TWO

The Early Years of the Build-up

Nitimur in vetitum semper cupimusque negata.

We always want the things which are forbidden to us,
and desire those which are refused.

Ovid

ALL THE EFFORT that went into the Lipezk venture was designed to ensure that flying formations were available if needed in the event of a general mobilisation. From 1925 onwards steps were being taken in the Reich Defence Ministry to build up a basic reserve of personnel and equipment. At first on an extremely modest scale since no-one could be sure of solving the problem of concealment. The Versailles treaty terms dealt particularly harshly with the development of aviation in Germany, until they were relaxed in an unexpected way.

After prolonged negotiations between the German government and representatives of the other signatories of the Treaty of Versailles, the restricting definitions were dropped and replaced, on May 22 1926, by a set of provisions, the so-called Pariser Verhandlungen. These maintained the strict ban on all military aviation but did permit the German aircraft industry to build, under rigorous inspection conditions, 'aircraft conforming to the aeronautical performance of current types of fighter aircraft', only in restricted numbers and for use exclusively for flying competition and record-breaking purposes.

This opened the door to an expansion of the aircraft industry in Germany, and a number of new aircraft firms came into being immediately. Only the most viable of these survived the fierce competition that ensued, and they—with government backing—constituted the core of the massive German aircraft industry of later years. It thus became possible to take the first tentative steps towards the creation, in secret, of an air force for national defence. It goes without saying that the German aircraft industry of those days lacked both the technical organisation and the ground staff necessary for the creation of an effective air defence system. There did exist, it is true, a pool of more or less modifiable civil aircraft and the civilian flying schools, from which reserves of a kind could be mobilized in an emergency, and this makeshift possibility was supplemented by certain measures which the Defence Ministry took in the latter half of the 1920s, including the setting up of a testing station registered under the cover-name of Fertigungs GmbH (Fabrication Limited) and run by the aeronautical branch of the army ordnance department. Its job was to examine and assess the designs and calculations submitted by aircraft manufacturing firms so as to ascertain whether or not they conformed to the specifications laid down by the air staffs of the higher commands of the army and of the navy. The requirements conveyed to the industry regarding military aircraft were specifically drafted with the aim of initiating the purposeful development of an effective air defence system with minimum wastage of the limited resources available. By the end of the 20s, the army ordnance department had given up altogether the practice of giving development order for particular types of aircraft to individual firms.

Nevertheless, soon after the conclusion of the Pariser Verhandlungen, the air staff of the naval higher command invited the industry to enter for the German Seaplane Competition 1926 at Warnemünde, offering a prize of 360,000 Marks (£32,000) for the winner. The object of the exercise was to net as large a number of advanced seaplane designs as possible. There were 17 entries from aircraft firms of which 10 eventually took part in the competition. The winner was Wolfgang von Gronau in an He 5a, with a Junkers W 33 as runner-up and a Heinkel He 24 biplane piloted by Dipl-Ing Spies in third place. This competition was of the greatest practical value. For instance, as a direct result of it, the firm of Heinkel was enabled to press on with the development that had its beginnings in the earlier HD 22 and 24 trainers and He 5 and He 9 reconnaissance types. In the case of Junkers, the competition led to the building of the W 33 and W 34 types, large numbers of which were produced for export.

The first invitation to tender issued by the Gruppe BSx (air section of the naval higher command) in 1926 constituted for the time being an exception, since the navy went over to procuring its equipment in the same way as the army ordnance department. For the testing of the tactical capabilities of the aircraft built by the various firms, the navy had to set up its own testing station, since Lipezk could only handle land-based aircraft, and the navy had rejected the use of seaplane facilities at Odessa on the Black Sea originally offered by Russia. So in 1926 Naval Captain Lochmann acquired the Caspar Works at Travemünde, an aircraft factory which had been closed down for lack of orders. In 1928 this outfit was transferred to the air defence branch of the naval higher command and named from then on Seaplane Experimental Station (SES) Travemünde. It was in fact equipped exclusively for tactical testing and was subsequently, under ex-Commander Moll, attached, for camouflaging reasons, to the German Airlines Federation.

The firm of Dornier was brought in to cope with flying boat development. The navy carried out extensive trials with the earliest Dornier WAL flying boats and also instigated the development of the Superwal, several of which were put into service. In 1927, the naval higher command gave Dornier the order to develop the Do X flying boat which was built in the firm's affiliated works at Altenrhein in Switzerland. This was to be a seaworthy experimental flying boat of maximum dimensions to be used, experimentally, as a long-range reconnaissance, mine-laying and torpedo-carrying aircraft.

The aircraft manufacturing firm of Rohrbach was also engaged in flying boat development, and built the Ro VII *Robbe* for the navy, which in turn led to the development of the two *Romar* aircraft for Lufthansa. The twin-hull flying boat ordered from Junkers never got beyond the drawing-board stage, for lack of finance.

The then novel idea of carrying aircraft on board ships was also put into practice in those early days. To this end, a ship-borne observation aircraft was ordered from and built by the firm of Heinkel. Both this observation aircraft, the He 60, and also the first single-seater fighter, the He 38, were designed for catapult launching, and Heinkel embarked simultaneously on the production of prototype catapulting equipment. The navy went on to order a floating dock equipped with catapulting gear for aircraft. This floating dock was also equipped with workshop facilities and designed to take aircraft up to the size of the giant Do X.

The operation of seaplane carrier-borne aircraft began with the collaboration of Hapag and Norddeutscher Lloyd. These shipping lines took naval personnel and aircraft on board their vessels cruising in Mediterranean and Northern waters. On these cruises the first practical tests were also carried out with the Kriwull towed glider. Work on armament, which was directed by Dipl-Ing Cornelius, resulted in the development, in collaboration with the firm of Örlikon, of a 2cm aircraft cannon with which the first firing tests in flight were carried out from a Wal flying boat.

The navy pressed on particularly actively and successfully with development in the field of WT communications, directed by Ing Bock. Extensive testing of direction-finding methods and equipment was also carried out from Travemünde, using a wide variety of aircraft.[1] The firms of Lorenz and Telefunken built the earliest modern aircraft wireless installations, to orders placed by the naval authorities. In order to test this equipment over long distances, two flights were undertaken with a three-engined Junkers G 24 and a long-range Heinkel aircraft, the He 10, over Lisbon and out as far as the Azores.

On aircraft engine development, which was directed with outstanding

[1] Following aircraft took part:

Junkers A 20 D–826	Rohrbach Ro VII D–926	Heinkel He 5b D–938
Junkers W 33 D–921	Rohrbach Ro VII D–927	Heinkel He/S 1 D–939
Junkers W 34 D–922	Heinkel HD 24 D–934	Udet U 13 D–945
L F G V 60 D–924	Heinkel HD 24 D–935	Gerbrecht W 3 unknown
L F G V 61 D–925	Heinkel He 5a D–937	

ability by Dipl-Ing Eisenlohr, the navy worked in conjunction with the appropriate section of the ordnance department and with the Defence Ministry. At the same time, the BSx Group was particularly active in promoting not only the development of engines for land-based aircraft but also the building of seaplane engines. An order for the first double-acting two-stroke Diesel engine was placed with the firm of MAN in Augsburg, and Daimler-Benz got the order to build an 800hp seaplane engine which was never in fact used to power aircraft, although some 20-30 of these engines were installed in speedboats and are said to have performed extremely well. It was on this failed seaplane engine that Daimler-Benz based the development of this firm's first diesel aircraft engine, the DB 602, which was used to power the airships LZ 129 (Hindenburg) and LZ 130 (Graf Zeppelin). On the basis of the preliminary work carried out for the navy, Daimler-Benz went on to develop the DB 600 engine. Under conditions of the greatest difficulty created by the necessity to operate in secret, further progress was made in the development of aerial torpedoes at Eckernförde, with the assistance of the naval torpedo testing station.

On assuming command of the Air Defence Group on October 1, 1929, Captain Zander was able to continue the expansion of the naval air arm which had been so successfully started by Captain Lahs. The period of flying training undergone by naval cadets prior to entry into the navy was extended to a full year to enable a higher standard of training to be achieved. Two-year courses were started at Warnemünde, under the camouflage designation of WT Experiments Command, to give young naval officers systematic thorough training as pilots and observers in seaplanes. The training of Engineer-Officers for the air force in two-year courses, and the training of flight mechanics started at the same time. Officers in the naval air arm were also required to take the fighter pilots' training course held at the German air base of Lipezk in Russia. At the same time, the ground organisation was brought up to the standard required by the naval air arm, through further improvements in, repairs to, and development of the existing seaplane and landplane bases and installations at Norderney, Wangerooge, Wilhelmshaven, Mariensiel, List, Holtenau, Travemünde, Warnemünde and Bug, and through the provision of new installations at the air-bases of Heligoland, Pillau and Nest, all within the limits set by the restricted resources available and by the necessity for concealment.

Aeronautical and engineering development was stepped up in 1929 as a result of the first regular invitations to tender for development contracts relating to military aircraft production and of growing investment in this field. In the years 1931 and 1932, the aircraft industry was able (with government backing) for the first time to go into a series production, on the smallest possible scale, of the He 59 multi-purpose seaplane, the He 38 single-seater fighter-seaplane and the He 42 trainer-seaplane. They were invaluable assets. Meanwhile, several Dornier Wal flying boats were obtained and the Heinkel He 51 (w) was developed. Also in 1931/32 the first seaplane tenders were built.

By the time Captain Zander handed over to Commander Wenninger as head of the Section on September 30, 1932, the framework of a naval air arm had been created as regards structure and ground organisation, training facilities, technical development and know-how gained through practical experience with the navy, so that as soon as the veil of secrecy was lifted and more resources became available it would immediately be possible, without losing any time on trials and experiments, to build up a large-scale and fully adequate naval air force.

On May 19, 1930, the chief of the higher command of the army, Lt-Col Felmy issued the order detailing the air force dispositions and requirements for the period 1931–37. Among other items, it was laid down that in the event of mobilisation (Case A), a reconnaissance squadron, two fighter squadrons and a night bomber squadron were to be put at the disposal of the Army Chief-of-Command, of each Army Higher Command (AOK) and each Corps Command (GenKdo). Thus, in all 22 squadrons would be needed to meet the most urgent demands of the emergency forces. This Order also made mention, for the first time, of the formation of the advertising squadrons. Finally, in 1932, specific detailed instructions were issued relating to the raising of a combat air force within the framework of a peace-time army. In this connection, the terms 'combat air force' and 'defence air force' were defined as implying that these forces were auxiliary to the army and the navy and therefore subordinate to the higher strategic command on land and at sea. This did not however preclude the possibility of army and navy air forces being required to serve in combined operations under a unified command. On the other hand, an air force constituting an independent arm under its own command would be incompatible with the proper function of a peace-time air force.

Apart from the already-mentioned tenders submitted in 1929, the firm of Heinkel developed, in the years 1930 and 1931, a long-range reconnaissance aircraft which received the type designation He 45 designed to have bomber capability, also a short-range observer and artillery-spotting aircraft, the He 46, and the He 51 fighter. The firm of Arado had tendered for fighter development contracts and built, one after the other, prototypes of the SD I, SD II, SD III and SSD I. None of these aircraft was up to international standard, so they were superseded by the Ar 64 fighter. Junkers brought out the K 47 and Dornier the Do 11. The K 47 was an all-metal, two-seater fighter designed and built in the Junkers branch factory in Sweden, and was at the time probably the most advanced aircraft of its kind. It had been developed as far back as 1928 and was built before the army department issued its specifications. In spite of the fact that this single-seater fighter was noted for its high performance figures and excellent handling—the pilots at Lipezk were fond of flying it—it was eliminated from the Reichswehr equipment schedule, not only because it had features which deviated from the specifications but also because in comparative flying tests the biplane types invariably proved superior to the K 47 in every respect. This was also the reason why the Ministry adhered to the conventional biplane principle of design in all future fighter aircraft.

The Do 11, on the other hand, was identical with the Do F freighter aircraft and was marked out for service as a bomber and long-range reconnaissance machine. The development of a bomber for the army was referred to in the 1927 army ordnance department procurement schedule as being under consideration. The Technical Requirements (Specifications), coded *Gronabo*[1] (standing for heavy night bomber), called for a high-wing monoplane with four engines, for long-range operation, a speed of 132mph, and an operational ceiling of 15,000 feet. To meet these requirements, Dornier developed the Do P. This action was undoubtedly due to official thinking on the subject of strategic warfare probably inspired by the theories advanced by the Italian air force General Douhet, and the fact that the air forces of other countries were forcing the pace in the development of multi-engined bombers.

The leading firms in the German aircraft industry, particularly Dornier, Junkers and Rohrbach, were perfectly capable of producing aircraft of four-engined night bomber type, but their capacity was insufficient to enable them to turn out heavy bombers in the numbers required in addition to the series production of commercial airline aircraft. The obligatory camouflaging would also have stood in the way. In view of all this, the army high command, after long hesitation, decided on the procurement of a two-engined medium bomber, and this led to the development of the two-engined Do 11. From the test results it was clear that this aircraft was far superior to the multi-engined makeshift bombers obtainable in an emergency by modifying existing civil aircraft.

As a result of the test programmes from 1932 onwards in connection with the plans for the creation of the army air force formations, the types chosen were the He 45 long-range reconnaissance, the He 46 short-range reconnaissance, the Ar 64 and He 51 fighter, and the Do 11 bomber aircraft, all of which stood up fully to comparison with the corresponding types in service in other countries. This achievement is greatly to the credit of the leadership of the armed forces and of the German aircraft industry in the face of all the prohibitions then in force and the hobbling effect of having to work under cover.

The products of the engine manufacturing industry, on the other hand, were not up to the standard reached in other countries, and this was due not only to the restrictions imposed by the Treaty of Versailles, but—more importantly—

[1] *Gronabo (Grossnachtbomber).*

to lack of the requisite raw materials.   From a discussion in 1932 between the head of the Russian air fleet, Alksnis, and the Inspector of Weapon Schools and the Air Force in the Reich Ministry of Defence, Major-General von Mittelberger, it appears that three types of aircraft engine had been short-listed by the Reichswehr at that time, namely the Siemens SH 22 which was selected for, among other types of aircraft, the Do 11, then an improved version of the BMW VI, and finally a so-called standard engine to be operated at less than full power on civil aircraft and at full output on military aircraft.   From a reported later conversation between a deputy commander-in-chief of the Russian air fleet, Meshenioff, and the head of the aeronautics department of the Army Office, Lt-Col Wimmer, it can be deduced that the engine in question was the BMW 12 which, by the autumn of 1932, had had several brake tests on the test-bed.   Otherwise it is noteworthy that the Reichswehr's interest was focussed on petrol engines and was only cursorily taking note of the Lufthansa testing of the Junkers Jumo 4 diesel engine.   In spite of the unsatisfactory power unit situation, the first bulk orders were placed starting in 1932, in the first instance for series of up to twenty aircraft of each type with the exception of the He 51 and the Do 11 production of which did not start till the financial year 1933.

On delivery, these series were handed over to the flying schools and the advertising squadrons[1] formed at the commencement of the 1930s.   All trained pilots and observers were grouped together in these squadrons.   The advertising squadrons were the first really operational flying formations to be incorporated in the Reich Army and had the additional function of marking targets at army manoeuvres, as well as reconnoitring for and maintaining contact between command posts.   The name was a hang-over from the undercover days when these aircraft were used for commercial advertising purposes. Apart from these three advertising squadrons based on Berlin-Staaken. Königsberg i. Pr. and Fürth near Nuremberg, a glider practising squadron was created.   The civilian flying schools, which possessed camouflaged military training facilities, were located at Brunswick, Jüterborg, Schleissheim near Munich, Würzburg and Warnemünde, the latter serving, as already mentioned, for seaplane training.   In addition, two squadrons of an army transport unit stationed at Rendsburg were formed into a stand-by pool from which NCOs and other ranks could be drawn for training and service as wireless operators, flight mechanics, air gunners and ground crew.   Altogether, the number of fully trained pilots available to the Reichswehr in 1933, to man the staffs and formations then to be set up, was of the order of 550.

In the course of the years 1920–33, the leadership of the Reichswehr had in every respect laid the foundation on which a peace-time air force could be further built up within the framework of a new peace-time army.   Part of the

[1] *Reklamestaffeln*—also Publicity Squadron.

job was a reshaping of the upper echelons of the air forces, for it had become clear in the preceding years that the air staffs of the army and navy commands needed to be combined for better co-ordination in matters of common concern. In November 1932, the head of the navy department indicated his readiness, with certain reservations, to collaborate on the working out of a joint combined command structure for the air forces. Then, on January 24, 1933, came the separation of the Air Inspectorate from the Weapon School Inspectorate to which the Air Inspectorate had up to then been subordinate and now became independent, though remaining under the *Truppenamt* (department of personnel administration). And on February 8, 1933, the Minister for the Armed Forces of the Reich, von Blomberg, ordered the setting up of the central air operations staff of the army and navy commands, under the disguising designation of *Luftschutzamt* (Air Raid Protection Department) in the Reich Ministry of Defence. The setting up of the *Luftschutzamt* was not effected as a result of the change in the political leadership of the German Reich on January 30, 1933, nor of Goering's appointment as Reich Commissioner of Aviation. Goering was from then on in charge of all branches of civil aviation, ARP and private aviation. The Reich Minister for the Armed Forces remained in charge of military aviation and of military air defence.

CHAPTER THREE

The Luftwaffe Takes Shape

In future no state will be able to win a war unless it has at its disposal a completely independent air force of such striking power that it can obtain absolute air supremacy in a very short space of time.
General Giulio Douhet

ON APRIL 27, 1933, Goering's *Reichskommissariat für die Luftfahrt* (Reich Inspectorate of Aviation) became the *Reichsluftfahrtministerium* (RLM) (Air Ministry of the Reich); then, with effect from May 15, 1933, the expected step was taken of bringing the whole of the elaborate military aviation outfit, that had hitherto been kept secret, into the sphere of control of the Air Ministry under the Air Minister, Hermann Goering. This was the first step towards the formation of an air force constituting an independent branch of the armed forces. From this time on, the RLM (the Air Ministry) was in over-all control of the organising and equipping of all air forces in Germany.

The renaming of the former *Luftschutzamt* (Air Defence Office) as *Luftkommandoamt* (Office of Air Command) had already indicated the intention to invest it with far-reaching powers, and was duly followed, on September 1, 1933, by a reorganisation of the RLM which involved making the Secretary of State for Air, Erhard Milch, directly subordinate to the Air Minister, Hermann Goering, who had been promoted to the rank of General of Infantry on the preceding day. Under them were ranged, in order, the Air Departments designated LA (Command), LP (General Purposes), LC (Technical), LD (Administration), LP (Personnel) and ZA (Co-ordination). The Secretary of State was to function as the Minister's deputy in all military matters and was put in charge of all officers in the Ministry. The LA was in fact nothing but the masked Air Force General Staff in which the work started by the *Reichswehr* was to be carried on. This included the elaboration of an independent air war strategy with which Goering had nothing to do and which held its own in spite of the fact that it ran counter to the ideas entertained in leading political circles.

One of the first measures taken by the new Air Minister was to set up flying formations. Whoever may have been the originator of the idea, the first fighter squadron was to be equipped with Italian Caproni CR 30 aircraft.

It was to be based at Rechlin.   For reasons unknown, however, the Italian fighters were never delivered, so that Goering's very first effort in this direction fell flat.

To avoid any further delay in mounting a fighter squadron, recourse to the Reichswehr's advertising flights was necessary, and with the aid of these, the establishment of the 132 fighter squadron at Döberitz near Berlin was started on April 1, 1934, under the command of Major Ritter von Greim.   This was the first flying formation to be set up under the new regime, and it was supplemented from units which had been in existence since 1933, namely the *Reklamefliegerabteilung* (Advertising Detachment) with its three squadrons based at Berlin-Staaken (subsequently transferred to Döberitz), Neuhausen near Königsberg in East Prussia and Fürth near Nuremberg, the Lufthansa auxiliary bomber squadron based at Berlin, the Navy's seaplane training squadron, and equipment supplied by the firm of Severa.

After April 1, 1934, the following units were formed as a beginning:

> 5 reconnaissance squadrons
> 3 fighter squadrons
> 5 bomber squadrons
> 2 auxiliary bomber groups
>   the stand-by unit at the disposal of the Ministry
> 1 squadron of naval reconnaissance aircraft
> 1 naval fighter squadron
> 1 multi-purpose seaplane squadron
> 1 air service towing plane squadron.

The fighter squadrons were equipped with Arado Ar 65 and He 51 machines. To these were added the first Heinkel He 50s as dive bombing trainers, since the setting up of a dive-bomber group had been ordered in October 1933.   For this reason, *Jagdgeschwader* 132 were given the task of providing not only fighter training but also dive-bomber training, and with the job of making preparations for the setting up of a further fighter group.

In the meantime, new training stations had been established on German soil to make up for the loss of the German air-base at Lipezk in Russia which Hitler had ordered to be evacuated, for ideological reasons, in the autumn of 1933.   One of the air cadets wrote from Lipezk on August 16, 1933:

'Today we had our official farewell party with Tomsen (the Russian station commander at Lipezk) and Dandorf.   We had a cold collation, eggs in mayonnaise, bouillon, chicken, pudding with fruit, and coffee, Vodka, liqueurs and strawberry-cup.   Even between the various courses there were lots of toasts and speeches, and singing of the Internationale and the Deutschlandlied, with cheering and expressions of hope that "such good relations" between our two countries might continue, and to this we had to empty our full glasses over and over again.'

After the closing down of Lipezk, the pilots were trained at Italian flying schools, but only as a temporary measure.

The general recovery which then set in everywhere in Germany also affected all branches of aviation, and it was planned to build, by September 30, 1935, the 4,021 aircraft needed to equip the new formations. The following is a list of the requirements scheduled at that time:

	Type	
150 bombers	Do 11	
222 bombers	Do 13, later Do 23	
450 auxiliary bombers	Ju 52/3m	
19 fighters	Ar 64	
85 fighters	Ar 65	
141 fighters	He 51	
14 naval fighters	He 51 W	
12 naval fighters	He 38	
320 long-range reconnaissance (F)	He 45	
270 short-range reconnaissance (H)	He 46	
51 dive-bombers	He 50	
81 naval reconnaissance	He 60	
21 l-range rec. flying boats	Do 16 Wal	
21 multi-purpose naval aircraft	He 59	
9 bombers	Do 17	
9 bombers	He 111	
3 bombers	Ju 86	
72 reconnaissance aircraft (K)	He 70	
4 flying boats	Do 18	

Of this total requirement, the aircraft industry had delivered approximately half by the end of the year.

The first 77 of the Do 11s and the first 193 of the Ju 52s went to the bomber formations at Tutow and Fassberg and the bomber training stations at Lechfeld and Prenzlau, while 19 Ar 64s and 80 Ar 65s went to 132 Fighter Squadron at Döberitz and the fighter training station at Schleissheim, 150 He 45s and He 46s to Brunswick and Hildesheim, and 27 He 60s, 16 Do Wals, 12 He 38s and 14 He 59s to the seaplane squadrons. The first four of the He 70s were also delivered by the end of 1934 (for the cover-names of the air stations, see Appendix C). If these numbers are compared with the figures for March 1, 1934, it will be seen that the front-line strength increased ten times between then and the end of the year.

The German aircraft industry was at that time engaged in an extensive programme of development and expansion, which meant that the production figures quoted could only be achieved by granting licences, i.e. enabling each firm to turn out any other firm's product immediately if called upon to do so. Firms converted to aircraft production were included in this comprehensive licensing scheme as well. In this way it proved possible to keep large-scale production of military aircraft going continuously at full capacity, without neglecting new military and civil aircraft development programmes.

At the same time, private flying was being developed on an unprecedented scale and on purposeful lines. Under the slogan, 'Germans—be air-minded', Goering enlisted the enthusiasm of the young for flying as a sport. There was a nation-wide network of gliding associations, for instance, affiliated to the German Aero-Club and the *Ring der Flieger*, and these organisations were merged to form the *Deutscher Luftsportverband* (DLV) which in its turn made way for the National Socialist Flying Corps (NSFK). On March 25, 1933, a wartime friend of Goering, Bruno Loerzer, was made President of the DLV which laid the foundation for a standardised system of pre-military flying training, and in April 1933 Goering put the active members of the DLV into a standard grey-blue uniform which in 1935 became the *Luftwaffe* uniform.

By decree dated February 26, 1935, with effect from March 1, Hitler made the *Reichsluftwaffe*, as it was then called, into an independent branch of the armed forces, the others being the *Reichsheer* (army) and the *Reichsmarine* (navy). The name *Reichsluftwaffe* was Hitler's choice, but it failed to catch on, and since the air force was invariably referred to as the *Luftwaffe*, this came to be officially recognised.

In March 1935, the air force came out into the open, its total strength comprising 20 land- and sea-based squadrons of aircraft, 20 land-plane and seaplane training stations, the Lufthansa auxiliary bomber squadrons and the stand-by unit of RLM. On March 14, 1935, 132 Fighter Squadron based at Döberitz-Damm was given the evocative title of *Jagdgeshwader Richthofen Nr. 2* (Richthofen Fighter Group No 2). In the same month, the *Wehrbefreiung* (declaring Germany sovereign in matters of national defence) was proclaimed by the publication of the 'Law relating to the establishment of the armed forces', while formations of the Richthofen Fighter Group staged a fly-past over Berlin in their Heinkel biplane machines. The purpose of this was to demonstrate the presence of a *Risikoflotte* (challenging air fleet) to clear the way for further rearmament which was then initiated by the proclamation of universal conscription. March 1 was declared Air Force Day, and was celebrated year by year thereafter with flying displays and parades. The days of camouflage and concealment were over and done with, and the *Luftwaffe* immediately set about increasing its strength by leaps and bounds. Recruits flooded in, from Lufthansa, from army and navy, and from the population at large.

From then on, everything considered necessary for the defence of Germany in the air was welded together in the *Luftwaffe* as an independent, integrated force.   Air intelligence and communications were from the outset under the direct control of the Air Ministry, since it was its job to maintain communications within the air force and between the air force and other branches of the armed forces and to channel essential information derived from a monitoring service.   The anti-aircraft defence force was officially integrated into the *Luftwaffe* on April 1, 1935, when the force comprised 29 AA batteries, the first unit having been re-formed in November 1933, at Wolfenbüttel, under the disguise name of Transport Detachment 6.

The front-line strength which in March 1935 comprised five reconnaissance squadrons, three fighter squadrons, five bomber squadrons, and three naval air squadrons, had grown to a total of 48 squadrons, that is to say had practically trebled in size by August 1, 1935.   The practice of awarding prestige names to individual groups was continued.   Thus, from April 3, 1935 on, Bomber Group I./154 at Fassberg was known as *Geschwader Boelke*, Dive-bomber Group I./162 *Schwerin*; an off-shoot of Richthofen 2 Group as *Geschwader Immelmann*, and from April 20, 1935, the new 134 Fighter Group as *Jagdgeschwader Horst Wessel Nr. 134.*

In the same year (1935), the reconnaissance squadrons were regrouped, according to whether they were long-range (F) or short-range (H), the former carrying out operational reconnaissance for the higher command and the latter serving in a general capacity in support of the army.   The long-range reconnaissance squadrons were equipped with Heinkel He 45s and the short-range reconnaissance squadrons with Heinkel He 46s.   Supplementary to the long-range reconnaissance squadrons, and forming a detachment of the RLM (Air Ministry) standby unit, there was a special-purpose squadron equipped with Heinkel He 70 reconnaissance aircraft and used for high altitude flying duties.   Later on, this squadron also served for high altitude testing and research missions, and, finally, directly under the Commander-in-Chief of the *Luftwaffe*, starting in peacetime conditions, on photographic reconnaissance missions over territory beyond the national frontiers of Germany.

In 1935 there were many complaints from within the flying formations, after initial assignments in connection with the Reich Party Rally at Nuremberg and following the Warnemünde air exercise, particularly from the crews of the Do 11s which, after certain modifications, were put into service with the bomber squadrons as Do 23s.   Dissatisfaction with this aircraft was justified since, even after reduction of the wing-span, the wing tips were very apt to whip in very bumpy weather conditions.   For air gunnery, on the other hand, the Do was preferred to the Ju 52.   The design of the defensive armament mounted in a retractable metal 'bucket' below the fuselage, aft of the under-carriage was unfortunate and caused a great deal of difficulty.   At high altitudes

(16,000ft) crews did not like manning the open gun-turrets. When fully laden, the aircraft were too slow and too cumbersome. Bitter complaints over the He 46 were often heard from the observers too.

The available equipment was not more and not less well up to the standard prevailing in 1932 when the *Reichswehr* were in control of military flying. The *Luftwaffe* had to make do with biplanes fitted with fixed landing gear and armed with two synchronised 7.9mm MGs in order to be able to keep up, at least quantitatively, with the formations' demands. Meanwhile everywhere else in the world the greatest efforts were being made to get away from the biplane principle and to replace it by the monoplane. Now the reconstituted *Luftwaffe* was given the opportunity to make this changeover faster than others could. The supply department of the Air Ministry, therefore, in the summer of 1934, invited tenders for the development of a fighter aircraft having the smallest possible airframe and equipped with the most powerful engine then available. Moreover, a speed of over 280mph was specified. Arado came forward with the Ar 80 designed by Walter Blume, Focke-Wulf with the Fw 159 designed by Kurt Tank, Heinkel with the He 112 and Bayerische Flugzeugwerke, of Augsburg, with the Bf 109 designed by Willy Messerschmitt.

Comparative flight tests with these four aircraft were carried out in October 1935, and of them the Bf 109 was clear favourite for selection as the future standard fighter for the *Luftwaffe*. Later, Heinkel made one more attempt, with the newly developed He 100, to compete against the Bf 109, but for various reasons this attempt also failed. The supply department of the Air Ministry stuck to its decision to equip the air force with one single type of fighter, and continued to do so even when, on Whit Sunday 1938, the He 100 V 2, fitted with a standard engine and with Udet at the controls, during a test flight beat the air speed record set up by the Italian Niclot by a margin of 50mph, attaining a top speed of 394.6mph. On March 30, 1939, Group-Captain Dieterle in a Heinkel He 100 V 8, reached 463.92mph, thereby setting up a new absolute speed record and bringing it, for the first time in the history of aviation, to Germany. This record was broken on April 26, 1939 by Messerschmitt's test pilot, Fritz Wendel, in an Me 209 V 1 with a speed of 469.22mph. Later it was found that the Messerschmitt 209 was purely a record-breaking aircraft and, on account of various troublesome flying characteristics, useless as a fighter aircraft.

Heinkel suffered a similar fate with his He 118 dive-bomber prototype. Away back in the days when the *Reichswehr* was making the running, dive-bombing was being tested as a tactical weapon at Lipezk, and it was recognised even then that precision bombing could only be achieved from an aircraft directed straight at the target in a steep dive. On the strength of this knowledge, the formation of the first-ever dive-bomber unit was ordered soon after the start of the disguised air force build-up. This unit was provided at first, for want of more suitable equipment, with the Heinkel He 50, a biplane capable of carrying a load of 250kg but incapable of attaining, in a power dive, a speed of more than 185mph which was too slow for dive-bombing. Although the then head of the development section of the supply department of the *Reichswehr*, Major Dr Ing Freiherr von Richthofen, expressed certain reservations regarding the dive-bomber, he nevertheless invited the aircraft industry to tender for a development project which led to the designing and building of the Henschel 123 and the Fieseler Fi 98. The Hs 123 was superior to the Fieseler in every respect, and it was selected to equip the first dive-bomber formations to go into service.

The second phase in the development of the dive-bomber was initiated by Udet as the first step taken by him after he was put in charge of the technical supply department (*Technisches Amt*). After that, a number of types was developed, Junkers producing the Ju 87, Arado the Ar 81, Blohm & Voss the Ha 137 and Heinkel the already mentioned He 118. They were all tested, in competition with each other, at Rechlin, in the summer of 1936, and although the He 118 was structurally superior to the others it was eliminated along with the Ar 81 and the Ha 137. The winner was the sturdy monoplane with the characteristic inverted-gull wings, the Ju 87. In 1938, the Ju 87 was adopted as standard equipment for the dive-bomber formations, while the Hs 123, which had served as second-string equipment for the *Immelmann* 162 dive-bomber group, was taken over as ground attack aircraft for use in the combat testing of personnel carried out by the instructor squadron.

Meanwhile nearly all the old-established aircraft manufacturing firms that existed at the start of 1933 had enlarged their plant or built branch factories. Aircraft development and series production was going at full steam, in the military and civilian sectors. Heinkel developed the He 111 out of the older He 70, Junkers developed the Ju 86 and Dornier came out with the Do 17. Performance was so good in the case of each of them that the air force authorities decided to have military versions developed from them. The He 111 and Ju 86 were intended to replace the Do 23 and the Ju 52 stop-gap bomber, while the Do 17, which was not quite what Lufthansa was looking for, was intended to become the high-speed bomber of the *Luftwaffe*, in the sense implied in the theory put forward by the Frenchman Camille Rougeron. None of these new types however could go into large-scale production until they had undergone more or less extensive field trials.

The year 1936 was dominated by the development and supply principles laid down by Major v Richthofen, e.g. to the effect that 'obtainable equipment of limited usefulness is better than no equipment' and that 'procurable equipment must be obtained as quickly as possible for any purpose, even if the equipment in question represents, for the time being, only an intermediate or emergency solution'. The *Luftwaffe* serving as a challenging air fleet should be permanently ready to go into action, and this meant that only equipment actually available was of decisive significance from the point of view of obtaining a looked-for success in a matter of a few hours.

At the end of 1935, by estimating the enemy's situation the higher command of the *Luftwaffe* saw in the first instance France and Poland as potential opponents, and in the second instance Belgium and Czechoslovakia. The possibility of a war on two fronts could thus not be ruled out. These were the kind of considerations that led to the formation of the challenging air fleet which was reinforced, stage by stage, according to the notions of warfare entertained for the time being by the *Luftwaffe* higher command. The concept underlying the creation of the *Luftwaffe* was completely keyed to the operational conduct of a war, that is to say a large number of two-engined (medium sized) level-flying bombers and single-engined dive-bombers were to fight the *Luftwaffe*'s independent battle against the enemy's war potential and give direct support to the operations of the army and of the navy. The territory of the Reich itself was to be protected, in the first instance, by powerful anti-aircraft units, so that fighter production could be restricted in favour of bomber production. An air war against Britain or Soviet Russia did not figure at all in this assessment of the situation, and air defence was thought of as being mainly a matter of combat formations. The two types of aircraft selected for this purpose were incompatible with the conduct of a strategic air war.

However, the strategic aspect was not left out of account. Although the German aircraft industry was working all out, so that any major development project would have engaged a considerable proportion of its capacity, nevertheless the chief of technical supply department, Col. Wimmer,[1] was empowered by the chief of air command at the Air Ministry,[2] Col. Wever, to place an order with the German aircraft industry for the development of a four-engined bomber. Dornier then built the Do 19 and Junkers the Ju 89, both four-engined types designed to meet the requirements put forward by the service authorities. Goering, when he visited the Junkers factory at Dessau in the spring of 1935, and inspected a mock-up of the Ju 89, expressed doubts of the soundness of this project. The War Minister, von Blomberg, on the other hand, when he visited the Dornier factory at Friedrichshafen, was favourably impressed with the Do 19 and said so. In any case, the upshot was that on April 29, 1937, work on the development of both these prototypes was stopped on orders from Goering, allegedly because they were powered with completely inadequate engines providing a top speed of barely 175mph and therefore did not meet the stipulated requirements. There were in fact no suitable engines available for such heavy aircraft, nor was there any prospect of suitable engines becoming available in the foreseeable future. Daimler Benz was engaged at

[1] Chief of the *Technisches Amt* Oberst Wimmer.
[2] *Luftkommandoamt.*

that time in developing a higher-power coupled engine designed to go into the Heinkel He 177 long-range bomber which had an airframe specially designed to take it. Immediately after cancellation of the Ju 89 and Do 19, the *Luftwaffe* higher command entrusted Ernst Heinkel with the development of a heavy bomber, thus proving conclusively that there was no intention of abandoning plans for a heavy bomber programme.

During the interval before the He 177 long-range bomber could go into series production, the *Luftwaffe* had to make do with the existing, horizontal-release medium bombers the range of which could only be increased by reducing the bomb-load carried. All the second generation aircraft, the Do 17, the Ju 88 and the He 111 were designed for medium-range operation and were therefore not capable, with an extra 2 tons of fuel on board, of carrying a sufficient bomb-load to compensate for the loss of accuracy inherent in horizontal release. The minimum bomb-load demanded by the General Staff was eight 250kg bombs per aircraft, as being the minimum with which any effective horizontal bombing could be achieved. Far more accurate bombing was achieved in the power-dive tests carried out by the training squadron. Attention therefore switched to the development of a bomber capable of carrying one or two bombs over long distances and releasing them in a power-dive on the target, and the *Luftwaffe* then called for a two-engined bomber with a crew of four, capable of a penetration radius of 1,000km (620 miles) and of going into the attack at a diving angle of up to 30deg. This specification of requirements reached the industry in the autumn of 1937 and had a lasting influence on all subsequent bomber development. The Junkers Ju 88 met the requirements; it had been developed on the basis of the requirement schedule issued in the spring of 1935 and was test-flown by Flugkapitän Kindermann, starting on December 21, 1936; it could attack from the horizontal, in low-level approach, and in both shallow and steep dive attacks. In dive-bombing trials with this machine 50 per cent of all bombs released fell within the target area of 50 metres diameter. As a long-range bomber the Ju 88 admittedly represented a compromise which the *Luftwaffe* regarded as of only short-term relevance. This state of affairs was basically due to the inadequacy of the available power-units which did in fact constitute the permanent Achilles heel of Germany's air rearmament.

Further expansion of the total strength of the *Luftwaffe* was achieved in 1936 by the so-called 'division of cells'[1] method of reorganising the combat units while at the same time bringing into front-line service the active training reserve already referred to, whereby the existing combat formations, now referred to as *Mutterverbände* (parent formations) were split up into two *Tochterstaffeln* (offspring squadrons). By mid-year, the new units were getting their full complement of personnel and equipment and becoming operational.

[1] *Zellteilung.*

Meanwhile, a large number of new air force stations and garrisons was being established all over Germany. At the start, building operations still had to be camouflaged. Later on, the scale of these operations became so great that it was pointed out in a report to the *Luftwaffe* General Staff that the location of the operational bases (*E-Häfen*) was known to foreign agencies, more particularly after an English commercial aircraft had made a forced landing at one of these bases allegedly to avoid a thunderstorm.

In this year again, two groups (*Geschwader*) had prestige names conferred on them.   152 Bomber Squadron received the appellation Hindenburg (*Kampfgeschwader Hindenburg Nr. 152*) and 253 Bomber Squadron that of General Wever (*Kampfgeschwader General Wever Nr. 253*).   General Wever, the first Chief-of-Staff of the *Luftwaffe*, when flying in a Heinkel 70 over Dresden Airport, crashed and was killed on June 3, 1936. He was followed, as air force Chief-of-Staff, by Lieutenant-General Kesselring.

CHAPTER FOUR

The Luftwaffe as Sabre-rattler

The German Luftwaffe *is passionately imbued with the urge to
defend the Fatherland to the utmost, and at the same time is equally
convinced that it will never be called upon to threaten the peace of
other countries.*

Hermann Goering

AFTER ITS DÉBUT in its political supporting rôle, with its opening exhibition
performances in connection with the Party Rally at Nuremberg and the
Harvest Festival on the Bückeberg in 1935, the *Luftwaffe* was made use of,
from then on, in this demonstrating capacity, at all public functions staged by
the political régime of the Third Reich. At the 1935 Bückeberg Harvest
Festival, Hitler outlined the task of the *Luftwaffe*, for the first time, in these
words: 'The German towns, the beautiful villages are protected, over them
watches the power of the nation, the armed force in the air'. And well did the
régime know how to parade this 'armed force in the air' effectively. The first
major part played by the *Luftwaffe* in this rôle, but at the same time as a fully
operational fighting force, was in connection with the remilitarisation of the
Rhineland, which started on March 7, 1936, when the units involved were
III./Jagdgeschwader 134 and I./Sturzkampfgeschwader 165. III./JG 134, led by
Captain Dinort, flew in from Lippstadt, circled over Cologne Cathedral
towards 12 noon, and then landed at their new home station Köln-Butzweilerhof
where each of the aircraft was armed with 1,000 rounds of ammunition, but
there was no preliminary gun and sight harmonisation. The staff and the 8 and
9 *Staffel* of the *III./JG 134* remained stationed at Cologne, while 7 *Staffel* was
transferred to Düsseldorf that same night. During the day, 165 Dive-Bomber
Group, operating from Kitzingen, moved two *Staffeln* to Frankfurt/Main
Airport and the third *Staffel* to Mannheim. Both Groups had only been in
existence for a relatively short time and were not of high fighting quality.

A different kind of proving in action awaited the *Luftwaffe* in the Spanish Civil
War, when General Franco appealed to the German government for military
support, in the first instance by ferrying some 15,000 Moroccan soldiers and
Spanish legionaries from Spanish Morocco to the mainland of Spain to provide
the initial basis for operations on Spanish soil. Hitler at once placed at Franco's

disposal the air transport capacity urgently required for this operation. On July 27, 1936, Flugkapitän Henke took off from Berlin-Tempelhof for Tetuan, with intermediate landing at Stuttgart, to initiate, on July 28, on a flight from Tetuan to Jerez de la Frontera, near Seville, with 22 Moroccan soldiers on board. This was the first air transport operation in the history of German military aviation. All in all, the first twenty Ju 52s, under the command of Ober-leutnant Rudolf Freiherr von Moreau, ferried 13,523 soldiers and 570,000lb of war material including 36 field guns and 127 machine-guns. The first 86 *Luftwaffe* volunteers to be shipped to Spain, along with six Heinkel He 51s and 20 AA guns for the protection and support of the airlift, set out on August 1, 1936, on board the SS *Usuramo*, under the command of Major von Scheele, disguised as tourists booked by the fictitious Union Travel Agency. After breaking the blockade, they disembarked at Cadiz in the night of 5/6 August. A hastily established Special Staff, with the code designation W, was entrusted with the carrying out of the Spanish mission, under the command of Lieutenant-General Wilberg who had gained extensive experience of disguised operations through his work at Lipezk in Russia.

On August 14, 1936, the first bombing attack by the *Luftwaffe* was carried out with a Ju 52 under the command of Freiherr von Moreau und Hoyos, in which the battleship *Jaime I* was put out of action by two direct hits from a height of 1,500ft. On August 21, 1936, the first air-lifted consignment of food, weighing two tons, was dropped over the beleaguered Alcazar of Toledo, after an unsuccessful attempt had been made the night before. From these small beginnings, German intervention in support of Franco was to grow. In November 1936 a further contingent of volunteers, 4,500 in all, sailed from the ports of Swinemünde and Stettin, disguised as participants in a 'winter exercise off Rügen'. This was in fact the very start of the Condor Legion, comprising —in November 1936—20 Junkers Ju 52s, 14 Heinkel He 51s, six Heinkel He 45s, one Heinkel He 59 and one Heinkel He 60 and subsequently supplemented by further aircraft until it finally comprised the following units:

BOMBER GRUPPE	K/88	30 Ju 52s
FIGHTER GRUPPE	J/88	3 *Staffeln* of He 51s
RECONN. STAFFEL	A/88	12 He 70s and a few He 45s
COASTAL STAFFEL	AS/88	9 He 59s and the He 60
AA DETACHMENT	F/88	
AIR SIGNAL COMMAND	LN/88	
OPERATIONS STAFF	S/88	

Commander-in-Chief of the Condor Legion was Major-General Sperrle, and Chief-of-Staff was Lt-Col Freiherr von Richthofen. Sperrle's successor, from November 1937 on, was Major-General Volkmann, who in turn was replaced, in November 1938, by Wolfram Freiherr von Richthofen who remained in command of the Condor Legion up to the conclusion of hostilities.

In the course of 1937, the flying formations were re-equipped, it having been found that the Heinkel He 70 did not come up to expectations either as a long-range reconnaissance aircraft or as a light bomber, and that the Heinkel He 51 was no match for the Ratas and Curtiss machines in aerial combat and could therefore only be used in ground attack operations. The Ju 52s were largely replaced, and otherwise supplemented by Heinkel He 111s and Dornier Do 17s, and the He 51s by Messerschmitt Bf 109s. This was when the Bf 109s first proved their worth in action, after their brilliant début at the Zürich International Air Show in July 1937, where they and the Do 17s were described by a foreign journalist as 'a piece of the fascinating German miracle'. In aerial combat, the Messerschmitt Bf 109 proved superior to all other existing types of fighter aircraft. This testing in the most rigorous operational conditions was undergone not only by the He 111, the Do 17 and the Bf 109, but also by the first of the Ju 87 dive-bombers to be developed by Junkers which were sent to Spain specifically for this purpose. Clear evidence of this is to be found in a passage contained in a report from the Rügen evaluation staff, which reads:

'The operational dive-bombing trials that have been in progress since September 1936, with three Junkers Ju 87 A–1s, have remained at an elementary stage owing to difficulties encountered in connection with the equipment.'

However, in October 1938, dive-bombing trials were resumed with the Ju 87 B–1, and this time better results were obtained. Bomber Group K/88 was responsible for carrying out these trials.

In the period from August 1936 to the end of October 1938, units of the Condor Legion destroyed 335 of their opponent's aircraft of which 277 were shot down in aerial combat and 58 by AA gunfire. The Rügen evaluation staff's report goes on to say:

'It did not prove possible to inflict lasting damage on or to put completely out of action any enemy air installations on the ground. It also proved impossible to knock out enemy air forces on the ground. The reason for this was the high degree of flexibility of the enemy formations and the effective use of dummy installations and aircraft mock-ups on the ground.'

The fighter pilot Hauptmann Lützow wrote, inter alia:

'The fact that we were fighting for a people other than our own, carrying out sorties deep into enemy territory, and the responsibility for irreplaceable, highly-qualified personnel, all this inhibited the keenness and natural élan of the German fighter pilot. He could only operate all-out when his own force's aircraft were in danger. The fact that we suffered only slight losses in spite of being outnumbered is due solely to the inadequate training and erratic leadership of our opponent's airmen, and to the greater speed of our own fighter aircraft, particularly in dive-bombing operations.'

The fighting achievements of the coastal squadron were characterised as thoroughly successful in 'operations against the Red Navy and Red Merchant Marine in Mediterranean waters'. The general conclusion drawn was that involvement in the air was never decisive because the available forces were inadequate. The most frequently successful operations were those carried out in direct support of land and sea operations, and they grew in significance as the tactics used became more precise.

In December 1938, the Condor Legion had at its disposal 40 He 111s, three Ju 87s, 45 Me 109s, five Do 17s, five He 45s and eight He 59s. The Spaniards had 146 and the Italians 134 aircraft in operation. In the course of the Civil War, between 1936 and 1939, the *Luftwaffe* lost in all 96 aircraft, about 40 of them through enemy action.

The *Luftwaffe* gained combat experience in Spain which could never have been gained by theoretical instruction, however well devised, nor by tactical exercises, however well planned. One example of how this experience was turned to practical account was the formation, immediately after the end of the Spanish Civil War, of a special headquarters staff having the designation *Fliegerführer zbV* (*zur besonderen Verfügung*—'for special duties'). A team of experts, led by Major-General von Richthofen, and joined later by the Fighter Command General Galland (as he later became), worked out guide-lines for the organization, training, and operation of ground-attack formations on the basis of the experience gained in Spain, with the aim of enabling two fighter-bomber *Geschwader* to be set up at an early date. They were equipped with He 51s, Hs 123s and He 45s most of which were later replaced by Hs 129s.

In the early part of February 1938, the *Luftwaffe* was once more reorganised to provide a more closely integrated chain of command. This constituted a first step towards the concentration of all available forces, and was followed, in February 1939, by a further, more radical reorganisation. The then existing seven *Luftkreisen*, on which the organisation of the *Luftwaffe* was originally based (after the subdivision of *Luftkreis IV* into *Luftkreis IV* and *VII*), were replaced by three *Luftwaffengruppenkommandos* and two *Luftwaffenkommandos* after which the higher command of the *Luftwaffe* was structured as follows:

The Air Ministry (RLM) was the supreme authority, headed by the *Reichminister der Luftfahrt und Oberbefehlshaber der Luftwaffe* (D.R.d.L. u. Ob.d.L.)— Air Minister and *Luftwaffe* C-in-C (officially abbreviated to The R.d.L. and

Ob.d.L.)—in the person of *Generalfeldmarschall* Hermann Goering, flanked by the Head of the Ministry Staff, *Major-General* Bodenschatz. The Minister's deputy was the Secretary of State for Air, *Generaloberst der Flieger* Milch, the Chief-of-Staff was *Lieut.-Gen.* Stumpff, the Chief of Air Defence was *General der Flakartillerie* Ruedel, and the Inspector-General of the *Luftwaffe* was *Lieut.-Gen.* Kuehl.

The General Staff was subdivided into Headquarters Staff, Organisational Staff and Training Staff. Other elements of the higher command were the Quartermaster-General, the Head of the Air Signal Command, the Head of the Medical Corps, the Air Force Academy and the Higher Air Force School.

The RLM comprised further the *Allgemeines Luftamt* (Air Offices), *Technisches Amt* (Technical Department), *Luftwaffenverwaltungsamt* (Administration Department), *Nachschubamt der Luftwaffe* (Supply Department), *Luftwaffenpersonalamt* (Personnel Department), and the *Zentralabteilung* (central or co-ordinating office). The Air Offices had under it the Air Service, Air Police, Meteorological, Air Traffic Control and Civil ARP Departments.

The Technical Department was responsible for issuing instructions regarding research, testing and procurement. The external branches of the Technical Department were the *Luftwaffe* (*Erprobungsstellen*) testing stations (*E-Stellen*) where prototypes were tested. The stations concerned were the following:

RECHLIN,	where airframes, engines, aircraft equipment, air gunnery and bomb-release equipment, and ground installations were tested;
TRAVEMÜNDE,	responsible for the testing of seaplanes and their equipment and armament;
TARNEWITZ,	for ballistics and measurement, sighting and aiming, guns and gun-mountings, ammunition and target simulation;
PEENEMÜNDE-WEST,	same as at Rechlin.

The Administration Department comprised Accounts, Pay, Uniform and Accommodation sections. The Supply Department was responsible for all *Luftwaffe* supplies. The Personnel Department dealt with all matters relating to officers, NCOs and other ranks, officials, clerks and workpeople. The Central Department was in control of the legal section and of diplomatic and press liaison.

The Inspector-General had ten *Luftwaffe* Inspectorates under him, which covered, respectively, reconnaissance and aerial photography, bombardment aviation, pursuit aviation, anti-aircraft gunnery, air safety and relevant equipment, motor transport, air signal (and communications), coastal, pilot training and education. The last-named Inspectorate was also in charge of the air force cadet schools located at Berlin-Gatow, Wildpark-Werder, Dresden-Klotzsche and Fürstenfeldbruck.

As already mentioned, the entire *Luftwaffe* was then organized: under three *Luftwaffengruppen* and two *Luftwaffenkommandos: Luftwaffengruppe 1 (East)* HQ was located in Berlin and commanded by *General der Flieger* Kesselring, *Luftwaffengruppe 2 (West)* HQ was located in Brunswick and commanded by *General der Flieger* Felmy, and *Luftwaffengruppe 3 (South)* HQ was located in Munich and commanded by *General der Flieger* Sperrle. The East Prussian Command HQ was located in Königsberg under *Lieut.-Gen.* Keller, and the Coastal Command HQ in Kiel under *General der Flieger* Zander.

At Army Supreme Command HQ there was the office of the Air Force General attached to the military C-in-C. Each *Luftwaffengruppenkommando* had under it a number of *Luftgaukommandos, Fliegerkorps* and (AA) *Flakkorps*. The size and composition of each *Luftwaffengruppe*, which constituted a complete small-scale *Luftwaffe*, varied according to the military tasks it was required to fulfil. Each *Luftgaukommando* was commanded by a General who, as the local *Luftwaffe C-in-C*, had under him the whole of the air defences, ground organisation, supply network and training and replacement units in his district.

By 1938, the number of operational *Gruppen* reached a total of 20 Short-range (H) and 19 Long-range (F) Reconnaissance *Staffeln*, 23 Fighter *Gruppen*, 30 (Bomber) *Kampfgruppen*, 9 Dive-bomber *Gruppen*, 5 Seaplane *Gruppen* together with 8 Multi-purpose-, 6 Reconnaissance-, 2 Carrier- and 2 Ship-board Aircraft *Staffeln*. The total of 243 *Staffeln* represented an increase of 30 *Staffeln* as compared with the preceding year, and meant that the plan set up in August 1935 had been completed by the autumn of 1938. Simultaneously with the formation of new operational *Gruppen*, the existing formations were equipped with the newest aircraft, starting in 1937 with the re-equipment of *Kampfgeschwader 255* stationed at Memmingen, with Dornier Do 17 Es, followed by the re-equipping of other bomber groups. In the end, more (bomber) *Kampfgeschwader* were equipped with Heinkel He 111s than with Dornier Do 17s. The long-range (F) reconnaissance *Staffeln* were relieved of their Heinkel He 45s and He 70s, which had performed disappointingly in the Spanish Civil War, and were likewise re-equipped with Dornier Do 17s. Some of the short-range (H) reconnaissance *Staffeln* were re-equipped with Henschel Hs 126s, while the Henschel 123s were replaced by Ju 87s. In 1937 a start was also made with the re-equipping of the fighter *Geschwader* with Messerschmitt Bf 109 machines. The designation *Bf*, standing for *Bayrische Flugzeugwerke*, was altered in 1938 to *Me*, the first two letters of the name Messerschmitt. The first formation to be re-equipped with the Bf 109 was *Jagdgeschwader Richthofen Nr. 132*. The formation of the Destroyer Formations equipped with the heavy two-engined Me 110 fighter aircraft did not take place until 1939.

The coastal (*Seefliegerstaffeln*) were re-equipped with the Dornier Do 18 flying boat for long-range reconnaissance duties, the Heinkel He 114 as carrier aircraft, and the He 115 as patrol and anti-shipping aircraft. For service with the carrier *Zeppelin*, the *Trägergruppe I./186* (Carrier Group) was formed at Burg near Magdeburg and equipped with Me 109s and Ju 87s.

The picture thus presented of a seemingly smooth and steady expansion must not be allowed to gloss over the fact that there were bottle-necks, as there had been in the past, particularly in aircraft engine output and in the production of synthetic fuels. On the other hand, clockwork precision was maintained in the build-up of AA forces and of the air signal units (Flak and Ln units), the former comprising, by the end of 1938, 20 regimental staffs, 46 AA *Abteilungen*, 14 light AA *Abteilungen*, 16 AA searchlight *Abteilungen*, five fortress AA *Abteilungen* and 24 cadre AA batteries, along with the AA gunnery school and the firing ranges. Each AA *Abteilung* comprised three batteries of four 8.8 or 10.5cm AA guns and two 2cm AA guns together with a 60cm searchlight unit. Each light AA *Abteilung* comprised one battery of nine 3.7cm AA guns and two batteries of 12 2cm AA guns each, together with one searchlight unit. The AA searchlight *Abteilung* each comprised three AA searchlight batteries of nine 150cm searchlights and six sonic detectors each. The five fortress AA *Abteilungen* constituted the cadre units of the Air Defence Zone West which was set up on June 1, 1938, extending for a depth of up to 60 kilometres along the Western frontier. This zone was studded with a coherent system of light and heavy AA batteries with effective range overlap, reinforced with balloon barrages in bad weather and searchlighting at night, with fighter patrols operating as well. By the end of 1938, the air signal command had attained a strength of 66 companies in three regiments and a number of *Abteilungen* with, in addition, the air signal school at Halle/Saale, the air signal training and testing regiment (Luftnachrichten Lehr- und Versuchsregiment) stationed at Köthen, the air signal unit of the *Luftwaffe* Higher Command HQ, 36 main-airfield signals companies, and 127 air force communication posts. Of particular interest in the records of this year is the fact that all flying Companies of the Ln (Signals) Regiments were provided with specially equipped Junkers Ju 52 aircraft which came to be dubbed *Nachrichten-Ju's* (Communication Ju's). With the aid of the most advanced communications equipment then available, these units ensured the operation of communication links with and between aircraft and formations operating from forward airfields.

In 1938, the *Luftwaffe* was given another opportunity to shine. On March 11, Hitler ordered the initiation of Operation Otto, involving massed troop movements over the frontier into Austria. Next day, while the troops on the march were accompanied by fighter and reconnaissance aircraft, bomber squadrons of *Kampfgeschwader 155* landed at Vienna-Aspern after dropping leaflets over the city, followed at short intervals by a large number of transport aircraft.

The merging of the Austrian air force with the *Luftwaffe* was started immediately, and completed on March 16, 1938, with the setting up of the *Luftwaffe* Command Austria under Major-General Löhr, with its HQ in Vienna.

Six months later, between October 1 and 10, 1938, 'Operation Green' was launched, with the movement of German troops into the Sudetenland, in which nearly 500 aircraft took part. The *Luftwaffe* Higher Command had taken precautions against any military resistance on the part of Czechoslovakia, including the alerting of an air fleet comprising 400 fighter, 600 bomber, 200 dive-bomber and ground attack and 30 reconnaissance aircraft, also preparations for committing, for the first time, the parachute units which had in the meantime been established and incorporated in the *Luftwaffe*. A battalion of paratroops was detailed to overpower the Czech frontier posts, while other paratroop units were to capture specified airfields, in case of need. For this purpose, airborne troop formations were put in a state of readiness in September 1938 at Oberschleissheim near Munich. The 7th Air Division had at its disposal, with the addition of the *Kampfgruppen* '*zbV*' *4, 5* and *6*, more than five complete *Lufttransportgruppen* (air transport groups) equipped with 250 Ju 52s in all. This massive standby did not in fact have to be put into operation, because in the event Czechoslovakia offered no resistance. Nevertheless the operation 'Exercise Freudenthal' was launched in order to give the para- and airborne troops operational experience. The *Kampfgruppen zbV* mentioned in this connection had arisen as a consequence of the re-equipping of the bomber formations with up-to-date aircraft, starting with *IV./Kampfgeschwader Hindenburg Nr 152* stationed at Fürstenwalde, which received the then available Junkers Ju 52 transport machines. This group later became the *Kampfgruppe zbV 1*, under the command of Lt-Col Morzik, which constituted the *Luftwaffe*'s first air transport group and was available for paratroop operations. As from April 1, 1938, this Group was also put under the command of the freight glider training unit. As an offshoot of *KG zbV 1*, the *KG zbV 2* was formed at Briest, followed in the late summer of 1938 by the formation of *KG zbV 4, 5* and *6* at Tutow, Fassberg and Lechfeld.

Hitler's intention, contrary to the promises he had himself given, of not contenting himself with the 'incorporation' of the Sudetenland, but of annexing Czechoslovakia as well, if necessary with force, prompted the *Luftwaffe* to take precautions against the possibility of Great Britain going to war with Germany. These precautions were taken in spite of Hitler's mistaken conviction that Great Britain would not intervene. General Felmy, who was entrusted with the carrying out of these preparations, submitted to Goering, in September 1938, a Memorandum on 'The conducting of air operations against England' in which he wrote, 'A war of destruction against England with the means at present available appears fruitless (*ausgeschlossen*)'.

On orders from Hitler, the *Luftwaffe* General Staff proceeded, in the autumn of 1938, to work out the air armament programme for the period autumn 1938 to autumn 1942, drawing conclusions from Felmy's memorandum as was clear from the planned setting up of thirteen *Seekampfgeschwader* under the title of 'Pirate Formations'. Of the total envisaged force of 58 squadrons, these thirteen were to be used exclusively for operations against naval targets, in which the enemy fleet was to be attacked with bombs and torpedoes, and mines laid in enemy waters. In addition, 30 *Kampfgeschwader* were to be used as a strategic air force against England, as is clear from the demand for as many Heinkel He 177 long-range bombers as possible. In contrast, 15 medium-bomber *Geschwader* were to be provided for the air war against France.

The detailed plans of the 'Concentrated Aircraft Procurement Programme' dated November 7, 1938 and signed by the Chief of Operations Staff, Colonel (*Oberst*) Jeschonnek, provided for the following equipment:

58 KAMPFGESCHWADER (Bomber-)	Ju 88 and He 177 (as many He 177s as possible at least sufficient for four Geschwader)
16 ZERSTÖRERGESCHWADER (Destroyer-)	Me 210, Bf 110 (as many Me 210s as possible, at least sufficient for 7–8 Geschwader)
8 STURZKAMPFGESCHWADER (Dive-bomber-)	Me 210 (Ju 87 Bs at time being established)
10 NAHAUFKLÄRER GRUPPEN (Short-range recon.-)	Hs 126 and Fw 189
10 FERNAUFKLÄRER STAFFELN (Long-range recon.-)	(Heer), (Army), Do 17 P and Z, and Fw 189
13 FERNAUFKLÄRER STAFFELN (Long-range recon.-)	(Ob.d.L.), (Air HQ), Ju 88 and He 177
1 SCHLACHTGESCHWADER (Ground attack-)	Fw 189
36 BORD- UND TRÄGERFLUGZEUGSTAFFELN (Shipboard and carrier aircraft-)	Bf 109 (Carrier), Ju 87 B, Fi 167 or Ar 195, Ar 196 (distribution worked out in consultation with Naval HQ 'Ob.d.M.')
4 TRANSPORTGESCHWADER (Transport-)	Ju 90 (if available in insufficient quantities, decision on substitute equipment deferred)
16 JAGDGESCHWADER (Fighter-)	Bf 109 and types developed therefrom.

All Staffeln to have an authorized allowance of twelve aircraft with the exception of fighter Staffeln which were to have eighteen aircraft each without increased personnel.

In a revised later schedule, the number of (dive-bomber) *Sturzkampfgeschwader*[1] was increased to 12. The total amounted to 20,000 aircraft. The AA artillery schedule comprised 2,500 heavy and 3,000 light batteries.

These figures were, without doubt, extremely high, and beyond the capability of the aircraft industry having regard to the raw materials situation then obtaining. The *Luftwaffe* General Staff must, however, have taken account of this possibility, since it indicated certain alternatives and margins. From the Concentrated Aircraft Procurement Programme it was also clearly deducible that an essential standardization, and the development of a long-range strategic bomber, were given high priority. The General Staff was not to blame for the fact that the aircraft industry failed to master the technological problem of producing the long-range bomber envisaged by Heinkel.

[1] Each Geschwader was divided into a staff unit and three or four Gruppen. Each Gruppe was divided into three Staffeln of nine (operational) and three (reserve) aircraft each.

CHAPTER FIVE

Flying into the Darkness

I will speak daggers . . . , but use none.
Hamlet

THE YEAR 1938 was the year of Hitler's most successful moves: the Austrian take-over, the occupation of the Sudetenland, the Munich give-away; all seemed to confirm his assumption of supreme command of the entire armed forces of the country on February 4, 1938. His star was at its zenith, and he immediately went to work to consolidate and extend his power. One of the steps to this end was the large-scale dismissal of commanding officers and service chiefs of proven merit to whom he took exception. By and large, the officer corps put up with this high-handed treatment. No voice was raised in protest. The *Wehrmacht* lost its identity and became a creature of the State.

Early in 1939, the operations staffs of the armed forces were ordered by Hitler to work out plans to overwhelm Czechoslovakia and to seize Danzig. This required a further concentration of forces which, in its turn, entailed a new re-organisation of the *Luftwaffe*. A Hitler decree of February 3, 1939, initiated a change-over in the higher command structure virtually from a peacetime to a wartime footing, designed to increase still further the *Luftwaffe*'s operational readiness and striking power. These measures were prompted not only by the new régime's foreign policy wiles but also by weaknesses in the leadership that were constantly coming to light in draft plans and studies undertaken by the *Luftwaffe* higher command. One of the decisive measures was to combine the offices of Secretary of State for Air and Inspector-General of the *Luftwaffe*, in the person of *Generaloberst* Milch. This meant that Milch was back in his former position, Deputy to the C-in-C of the *Luftwaffe* and as such, superior in the chain of command, to *Generalluftzeugmeister* Udet, to the air defence chief General Stumpff, to the chief of training services Lt-Gen Kühl, and to the Air Signals Command chief Major-Gen Martini, and also in charge of the Central Department of the Ministry. The office of Chief of General Staff, previously held by General Stumpf, was given to Col Jeschonnek who up to then had been chief of the operations staff section of the General Staff.

A further major step in the re-organisation was the abolition of the *Luftwaffe* Coastal Air Force Command and the simultaneous creation of the new post of *Luftwaffe* General attached to the Navy C-in-C, who then took charge of the coastal air forces. The greater part of the flying formations were organised into seven *Fliegerdivisionen* and these into three *Luftflotten*. The East Prussia air force remained a separate entity because of its geographical isolation, and Lt-Gen Wimmer was appointed its C-in-C, The Austrian air force command likewise remained independent for the time being. Maj-Gen Geisler became C-in-C Coastal Air Forces. In the spring of 1939, the Air Divisions and their commanders were as follows:

> 1st Air Division, Berlin, Lt-Gen Grauert
> 2nd Air Division, Dresden, Maj-Gen Loerzer
> 3rd Air Division, Münster, Maj-Gen Putzier
> 4th Air Division, Brunswick, Air Force General Keller
> 5th Air Division, Munich, Maj-Gen Ritter von Greim
> 6th Air Division, Frankfurt/Main, Maj-Gen Dessloch
> 7th Air Division, Berlin, Maj-Gen Student
> Training Division, Greifswald, Lt-Gen Förster
> Air Defence Zone West, Lt-Gen Kitzinger.

The new organisation was put to the test for the first time in connection with the occupation of Czechoslovakia which began on March 15, 1939. The 1st and 3rd *Luftflotten* and the Austrian air force command were detailed to operate in support of the army groups involved, but were grounded on the first day by bad weather and only able to take part in the operation after the weather had improved. On March 17, hundreds of aircraft staged a fly-past over the city of Prague. Immediately after this operation, the air force command Austria, the formations in Silesia and those in Bohemia and Moravia were merged to form the 4th *Luftflotte*.

Only a week after the occupation of Prague, Lithuania offered to return to the German *Reich* the District of Memel which she had occupied since 1923. On March 23, 1939, units of East Prussia Command crossed the Lithuanian frontier and circled for an hour over Memel, and on the afternoon of the same day a fly-past was held over the District of Memel.

At this juncture a turning-point was reached in the history of Europe and in international relations. The policy of appeasement gave way to the policy of containment. Hitler first reacted on the home front, by ordering the *Wehrmacht* to work out, within the framework of the usual project studies, plans for 'Operation White' (for the destruction of the Polish armed forces) so that it could be launched at any time from August 1939 onwards.

For the *Luftwaffe*, a map-exercise lasting for several days was laid on under the code-name 'General Staff Excursion 1939' (*Generalstabsreise 1939*) which contained, in addition to the 'Map Study 1939', the deployment and battle directives for 'Operation White'. The map exercise related exclusively to the air attack on Poland, designed to destroy the Polish air forces on the ground in a series of lightning raids. Only after this had been achieved were the *Luftwaffe* forces to be used in support of the military operations on the ground. This was a general instruction which figured in the chapter of the Air Force Regulations on 'Conduct of Air War' ((LDv 16) (*LDv* = *Luftwaffendienst-vorschrift*). In March 1939, the aggregate flying formation strength of the *Luftwaffe* totalled 83 *Gruppen* with 254 *Staffeln*, and three months later, on July 1, 1939, the number of *Staffeln* had risen to 276, comprising

55 reconnaissance squadrons
13 staff squadrons
90 bomber squadrons
27 dive bomber squadrons
40 fighter squadrons
27 pursuit-interceptor squadrons
3 ground attack squadrons
1 weather reconnaissance squadron
20 naval air force squadrons (including 1 rescue squadron)

276 squadrons, excluding two LN100 squadrons and the transport squadrons.

The re-organisation of the *Luftwaffe* entailed the adoption, as from May 1, 1939, of a new system of numerical designation of the various units. The *Geschwader* of *Luftflotte 1* were allotted the numbers 1 to 25, those of *Luftflotte 2* the numbers 26 to 50, those of *Luftflotte 3* the numbers 51 to 75, and those of *Luftflotte 4* the numbers 76 to 100.

Owing to the threat of war, and in the course of the consequential creeping mobilisation, the setting up of several fighter formations was accelerated, with the result that the number of front-line *Staffeln* grew to 302 by the end of August 1939, which was the strength at the outbreak of the war. The breakdown into categories and types of aircraft was a shown overleaf.

According to the figures published by the military records office at Freiburg,[1] out of the 4,093 front-line aircraft available at the start of the war, 3,646 were ready for immediate action, representing an effectiveness rate of 90 per cent.

The above-mentioned 18 Ju 88s pertained to a *Erprobungsgruppe*, and were stationed at Rechlin. At the start of the war, this test group of Ju 88s was led by Captain Pohle and was incorporated in *Luftflotte 2* as I./KG 25, later re-designated as I./KG 30. The figure of 552 transport aircraft comprised not only the machines pertaining to *KG zbV 1* and *2*, but also the aircraft stationed at the training establishments which would have immediately formed further

[1] *Militärgeschichtliches Forschungsamt* at Freiburg.

LG zbVs in the event of mobilisation. The previously formed ground attack groups *zbV 4, 5* and *6* were disbanded after the end of the Sudetenland episode. Of the Me 110 destroyers, only 95 were ready for immediate action at the start of the war; these were the aircraft with which Goering wished to protect his bombers during sorties. However, these heavy fighters had a penetration depth of, at the most, only 450km (280 miles) and were therefore unsuitable as fighter escort machines. Consequently, the General Staff cried out for the development of an escort fighter (destroyer) capable of penetrating to a depth of 1,000km (620 miles) with another half-hour's combat time in hand. The listed 313 Me 109 Cs and Ds were somewhat more heavily armed than the day-fighters and constituted no more than a makeshift answer to the problem.

LONG-RANGE RECONNAISSANCE	Do 17		257 aircraft
SHORT-RANGE RECONNAISSANCE	He 45	14	
	He 46	65	356 aircraft
	Hs 126	275	
DIVE-BOMBING	Ju 87		366 (incl. carrier-borne)
BOMBER	He 111 H	400	
	He 111 P	349	
	He 111 E	38	
	Do 17 Z	212	1,176 aircraft
	Do 17 E	119	
	Do 17 M	40	
	Ju 88	18	
GROUND ATTACK	Hs 123		40 aircraft
TRANSPORT	Ju 52		552 aircraft
DESTROYER (HEAVY FIGHTER)	Me 110 C	68	
	Me 110 D	27	408 aircraft
	Me 109 C	36	
	Me 109 D	277	
DAY- AND NIGHT-FIGHTER	Me 109 D	112	(incl. carrier)
	Me 109 E	631	771 aircraft
	Ar 68	28	
SEAPLANES AND FLYING BOATS	He 59		
	He 60		167 aircraft
	He 115		
	Do 18		

Total 4,093 aircraft

The 28 Arado Ar 68s listed among the day-fighters were temporarily incorporated in the two night-fighter *Staffeln*.

On July 1, 1939, the AA artillery comprised 21 regimental staffs, 46 AA detachments (*Abteilungen*), 17 searchlight detachments, 14 front-line AA detachments, and five fortress flak detachments. At the outbreak of the war, these units possessed 2,600 heavy guns, 6,700 light and medium-heavy guns, 1,700 flak searchlights of 59in diameter, and 1,300 of 24in diameter. The heavy gun types were 88mm Flak 18s, Flak 36s, and Flak 37s; the medium-heavy gun types were 37mm Flak 18s and Flak 36s; the light guns were 20mm Flak 30s. In addition, 105mm Flak 38s were undergoing trials.

The air signals corps had grown by July 1, 1939, to three communications and signals regiments which served as signal corps at *Luftflottenkommandos*. Then there was the I/Air Intelligence and Signal Regiment No 4 attached to *Luftflottenkommando* 4 Austria, and the Air Intelligence and Signals Detachment[1] No 6 stationed in East Prussia. The Air Region (*Luftgau*) HQs had their own air intelligence and signals regiments, and the Higher Command was in direct charge of the air signals and communications training centres, the LNS[2] at Halle-Saale, and the air signals special training and testing regiment[3] stationed at Köthen which had two flying squadrons at its disposal after the establishment of Air Communications and Signals Detachment No 100 (LN 100) in the winter of 1938/39. These squadrons were engaged on the trying out of W/T and navigation techniques used by the flying formations and were later used as navigation and pathfinding formation on target-spotting missions, for which purpose Ju 52s and He 111s were available. These squadrons and the monitoring units were top secret. At this time, the Air Signals Corps ordered an omnidirectional radio range to give improved position and direction finding on long-range flights. As far as Radar was concerned, the Signals/ Communication Training and Investigating Regiment was provided with a set of Freya equipment by the Navy after the occupation of Czechoslovakia where it was used for observation of the air space over Czechoslovak territory. Two further sets of Freya radar equipment were available to the air signals command at the start of the war.

The paratroops constituted a *Luftwaffe* task force and comprised, on August 1, 1939, five battalions totalling twenty companies, namely the 1st, 2nd and 3rd Bns of the Paratroop Regt No 1, and the 1st and 2nd Bns of the Paratroop Regt No 2. Transport was by the two ground attack groups (*KG*) *zbV* 1 and 2 consisting of eight transport squadrons in all.

The ground organisation comprised, on July 1, 1939, 197 land and sea air force stations, six seaplane bases and 19 other military airfields, as well as

[1] *Luftnachrichtenabteilung* (today: *Fernmeldeabteilung*).
[2] LNS—*Luftnachrichtenschule*.
[3] *Luftnachrichten Lehr- und Versuchsregiment*.

extensive supply and maintenance services for heavy equipment and aircraft, for armament and ammunition, for motor transport and for fuel.

Air force medical services comprised 10 air region medical detachments, 35 medical examination stations and four *Luftwaffe* hospitals.

The training establishment comprised 23 air training regiments and two independent battalions, along with 18 flying schools Grades A/B and C, seaplane flying schools, 10 air gunnery schools, aerial photography school, bombing school, torpedo school, parachuting school and a number of ground crew training schools.

In June 1939, the personnel strength of the *Luftwaffe* totalled 332,000 men (12,000 officers, 320,000 NCOs and other ranks). In August 1939, before mobilisation started, the flying and paratroop forces numbered 208,000 men, flak artillery 107,000 and intelligence and communications personnel 58,000 men. Flying personnel alone, i.e. pilots, navigators, W/T operators and flight mechanics, numbered 20,000.

Pilot training was carried out at the A/B and C Grade schools, the former using aircraft having a maximum take-off weight of 5,000kg (11,000lb), and the latter aircraft having appropriately higher take-off weight. The A1/A2 trainers used were the Klemm KL 25 and KL 35, Bücker 131 (*Jungmann*), Focke-Wulf Fw 44 (*Stieglitz*—Plover), and Heinkel He 72 (*Kadett*). The B1 trainers used were the Arado 66c, the Gotha 145, the Arado 76 and the Focke-Wulf Fw 56 (*Stösser*), the two last-mentioned types being mainly used for aerobatic training. The B2 trainers used were the Junkers W33 and W34, as well as the Focke-Wulf Fw 58 (*Weihe*), the latter being the transitional type with which training at the C schools started where the other types used were the Junkers Ju 86 and Ju 52/3m and the Heinkel He 111. Initial training at the seaplane schools was more particularly on Heinkel He 42s. Before a pilot could be posted to a flying unit, he had to hold the *Luftwaffe* Pilot's Licence which covered daytime, night-time and aerobatic flying proficiency, and navigational ability up to the stage of being able to traverse small-scale bad weather areas, and to return to base after a flight in triangular course under visual flight rules. Pilots with these qualifications were then passed on to the gunnery schools for training on single-engined reconnaissance, dive-bombing and fighter aircraft operating in formation. Only after completing this training was a pilot qualified to fly K-type (i.e. combat) aircraft. Pilots of multi-engined aircraft, after completing the A/B training course, went on first to the C Grade school to qualify for the ELF[1] Licence (extended *Luftwaffe* pilot's licence) entitling them to fly aircraft with an all-up weight in excess of 5,000kg (11,000lb). To qualify for the ELF-2 Licence, they then had to pass through a blind-flying training course, involving at least 20,000km (12,500 miles) of overland flying, 8,000km (5,000 miles) of it as pilot on B2 aircraft and

[1] ELF—*Erweiterter Luftwaffenflugzeugführerschein.*

the remainder as 2nd pilot on C aircraft. This was followed by intensive navigational training involving long-distance flights on radio and celestial navigation. 'The training for the blind-flying C pilot's licence was the longest, most costly, most complicated, and from the point of view of wartime operational effectiveness most important aspect of the entire air training process', to quote the retired Air Force General Kreipe in a treatise he wrote on the subject of the training of the *Luftwaffe*. The training of navigators, W/T operators, and flight mechanics was carried out in the appropriate specialised schools. Navigational training took six months, W/T operator training a year. Pilot test and examination results were assessed by aviation experts of the *Luftwaffe* who were flying officers of outstanding merit. At the gunnery schools, crews were assembled to carry out plotted flights, by day and by night, formation flying and bombing exercises at various altitudes. These crews then remained together after posting. Fighter pilots were trained in dog-fighting tactics, and learned to control their machines in all attitudes and flying conditions. Reconnaissance pilots were specially trained to supply operational HQs with satisfactory data in all weather conditions.

Of the total number of pilots holding the ELF Licence by 1939 about one-quarter had successfully passed the blind-flying course. When the war started, there were 1,300 bomber crews, 160 long-range reconnaissance crews, 150 seaplane crews and 450 transport aircraft crews available. Each crew consisted of pilot, navigator, W/T operator and flight mechanic. These 2,460 fully qualified front-line air crews could be supplemented by 1,500 crews from the gunnery schools, so that the effective total of air crews available when war broke out was approximately 3,960, with the reservation that not all pilots from the gunnery schools[1] held the ELF Licence.

Regarding the general state of training, the Chief of General Staff, Col Jeschonnek, on the occasion of the plan exercise conducted under the code name of 'General Staff Excursion 1939', used these words:

'Am worried that we are making such slow progress with the further development of tactics. The fault lies with the lack of fully experienced formations to push development forward. The *Luftwaffe* Technical Development Flying Division (Lehr Division) cannot cope with the problem unaided.'

Major-General Ritter von Pohl added:

'Let us hope, then, that we don't get the wrong ideas? We must face up to the fact that we have to fight with moderately well trained formations.'

[1] *Waffen Schule* (weapon's school).

The clear assessment of the situation by the Air Staff was completely ignored by the political leadership, for whom only the concrete facts and figures meant anything, the availability of some 370,000 professional personnel, volunteers and conscripts, 4,000 combat aircraft, and countless thousands of AA guns of all calibres. So it came about that Operation White was launched by the political leadership at a time when the *Luftwaffe* was fully engaged in the process of building up and re-arming, a process which could, at best, not be completed before 1942. On August 1, 1939, the *Luftwaffe* was no more than an operational risk-force, although capable certainly of coping with any operation, within a limited war framework, directed against any country bordering on Germany. But in the opinion of its Air Staff at that time, the *Luftwaffe* was not yet equal to conducting an air war overseas and carrying out strategic air attacks on targets in Britain. This conviction on the part of the Air Staff was, moreover, borne out by the conclusions drawn from the map exercise carried out by *Luftflottenkommando 2*. In spite of all this, the launching of Operation White became bitter fact on September 1, 1939. A mistaken assessment of what England's and France's attitude and reaction would be, was to trigger off the greatest tragedy in recent European history. A tragedy no less for the *Luftwaffe* too, with a global war on its hands which it was unprepared to face, and destined, as it was, to go down to defeat, out-numbered, after super-human efforts and in spite of the heroism of its individual members.

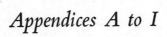

Appendices A to I

Appendix A

Structure of Organisation for Co-operation between the Reichswehr and Red Army*

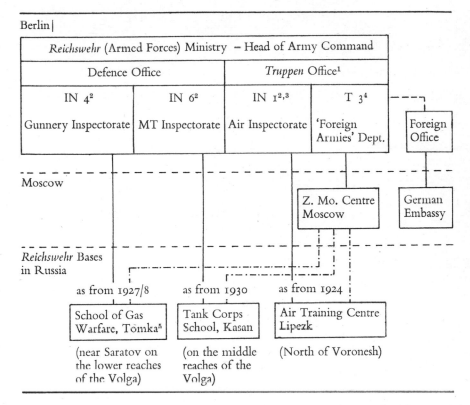

Berlin|

Reichswehr (Armed Forces) Ministry – Head of Army Command				
Defence Office		*Truppen* Office[1]		
IN 4[2]	IN 6[2]	IN 1[2,3]	T 3[4]	Foreign Office
Gunnery Inspectorate	MT Inspectorate	Air Inspectorate	'Foreign Armies' Dept.	

Moscow

Z. Mo. Centre Moscow	German Embassy

Reichswehr Bases in Russia

as from 1927/8	as from 1930	as from 1924
School of Gas Warfare, Tomka[5]	Tank Corps School, Kasan	Air Training Centre Lipezk
(near Saratov on the lower reaches of the Volga)	(on the middle reaches of the Volga)	(North of Voronesh)

Key ·—·—·— Territorially subordinate
– – – – Liaison
——— Directly subordinate

NOTES

(1) Head of Personnel Office was at same time illicit Chief of General Staff.
(2) IN 4, IN 6, IN 1: organised and set up bases, issued technical and service instructions relating to training and testing, provided finance, in the present instance under the so-called 'blue budget'.
(3) IN 1 = Army Command Inspectorate of Weapons Schools and Air Forces.
(4) T 3 = Central Department for Russian Affairs (policy on co-operation).
(5) Tomka was an imaginary place-name for reasons of concealment.
  * Named after ex-Air Force General Helm Speidel.

Appendix B

Aircraft Stock of the German Air
Training School at Lipezk/Russia

Actual stock of the aircraft on October 1, 1929:

A SINGLE-SEAT FIGHTER

    (1) 43 Fokker D XIII (Serial Nos.: 4599; 4600; 4601; 4603–4610; 4625; 4627;
                            4687–4690; 4692–4696; 4698; 4700; 4702–4706 and 4865)
    (2) 2 Fokker D VII (Without Serial No.)

B MULTI-SEATER

    (3) 1 Heinkel HD 21 (Serial No. 6)
    (4) 6 Heinkel HD 17 (Serial Nos. 239–244)
    (5) 1 Junkers A 20/35 (Serial No. 878)
    (6) 1 Junkers F 13 (Serial No. 572)
    (7) 6 Albatros L 76 (Serial Nos.: 10102; 10103; 10122–10125)
    (8) 6 Albatros L 78 (Serial Nos.: 10151–10156)

Appendix C

Code-designations of the Luftwaffen units during the activation period (April 12, 1934)

NAME OF THE LUFTWAFFEN AIRFIELD	COMPETENT CODE-DESIGNATION
Brandenburg	*Reparaturwerkstatt und Ersatzteillager der Reichsbahn (Frachtflugstrecken)*
Braunschweig	*Deutsche Verkehrsfliegerschule (DVS)*
Bug	*Nautische Vermessungsabteilung*
Cassel	*Luftbildlandesvermessung Westdeutschland*
Celle	*Erprobungsstelle der deutschen Versuchsanstallt für Luftfahrt (DVL)*
Cottbus	*DVL*
Döberitz	*Reklamestaffel Mitteldeutschland*
Erfurt	*Depot der Luftverkehrs AG Niedersachsen*
Fassberg	*Hanseatische Fliegerschule*
Fürth	*Reklamestaffel Süddeutschland*
Gersthofen	*Süddeutsche Lufthansa GmbH (Gebirgsschule)*
Göppingen	*Luftbildvermessung*
Gotha	*Reklame—Abteilungsschule*
Hildesheim	*Deutsche Luftfahrt GmbH*
Holtenau	*Luftdienst eV*
	Luftverkehr Schleswig-Holstein GmbH
Ingolstadt	*Lager der Süddeutschen Lufthansa A-G*
Jüterbog	*Technische Schule*
	Ersatzteillager der DVS GmbH
Kitzingen	*DVL*
Königsberg	*Lager der Luftverkehr Ostpreußen GmbH*
Lechfeld	*Hohenflugzentrale des Deutschen Flugwetterdienstes*
Liegnitz	*Depot der Schlesischen Luftverkehrs AG*
List	*DVS*
Magdeburg	*Reichsbahnfrachtflugzentrale*
Münster	*Flugwetterdienst Westdeutschland*
Neu-Brandenburg	*Lager der Luftverkehr Pommern GmbH*
Neuhausen	*Reklamestaffel Ostdeutschland*
Neuruppin	*DVS*
Norderney	*Luftdienst eV*
Pattensen	*Depot der Luftverkehrs AG Niedersachsen*
Prenzlau	*Forst- und landwirtschaftliches Flugversuchs-Institut*
Querfurt	*Lufttransportzentrale der Reichsautobahn*
Quedlinburg	*Fliegerlager des Freiwilligen Arbeitsdienstes*
Schleissheim	*DVS*
Seligenstadt	*DVL*
Stendal	*Depot der Luftverkehrsgesellschaft Brandenburg*
Stralsund	*Küstenwetterdienstzentrale Ostsee*
Tutow	*Funkpeilversuchsinstitut des Reichsstandes der Industrie, Gr. 9*

Ulm	*Lager der Süddeutschen Lufthansa A-G*
Warnemünde	*DVS*
Wilhelmshaven	*Küstenwetterdienstzentrale Nordsee*
Würzburg	*Deutsche Luftfahrt GmbH*
Wustrow	*Truppenübungsplatz*

Appendix D

Designation of *Luftwaffe* Units and Aircraft and Unit Markings (position in May 1936)

A *Geschwader*
A *Geschwader* consisted, as a rule, of:

1 *Geschwader* Staff having	4 aircraft
3 *Gruppen* Staffs having 3 aircraft each =	9 aircraft
9 *Staffeln* having 9 aircraft each	= 81 aircraft
Total	94 aircraft

A *Gruppe* comprised three *Staffeln*; a *Staffel* comprised three *Ketten* and a *Kette* had three aircraft.

B The *Geschwader* designations consisted of three digits, of which the first digit stood for the unit's number in the *Luftkreis* (Air District) concerned, while the second digit represented the type of the unit, and the third digit was the number of the *Luftkreis*. Thus *Jagdgeschwader 132* was the 1st Fighter unit of Luftkreis II. As the second digit, 1 = Short-range (H) Reconnaissance; 2 = Long-range (F) Reconnaissance; 3 = Fighter; 4 = (Heavy Fighter); 5 = Bomber; 6 = Dive-Bomber; 7 = Air Transport; and 8 = Multi-purpose aircraft. As the third digit, 1 = Luftkreis I, Königsberg i.Pr.; 2 = Luftkreis II, Berlin; 3 = Luftkreis III, Dresden; 4 = Luftkreis IV, Münster; 5 = Luftkreis V, Munich; and 6 = Luftkreis VI, Kiel.

C Aircraft Markings
All militarily equipped aircraft, i.e. those having permanently built-in armament or fitted with bomb release gear, bore the arm and service insignia of the *Balkenkreuz* with white bordering, and in addition numbers and letters for identification, as follows: 1st digit = *Luftkreis No.*; 2nd digit = Unit No.; (Balkenkreuz |); 1st letter = number of aircraft within *Staffel*; 3rd digit = *Gruppen* No. within *Geschwader* and 4th digit = Staffel No. within Geschwader. For instance, a marking which read 21 + B38 meant the second aircraft (B = 2) of the eighth *Staffel* in the third *Gruppe* of the first unit pertaining to *Luftkreis II*.

D The reconnaissance *Staffeln* of a K Group were assigned the *Gruppen* designation O and instead of a numerical *Staffel* designation the letter K. For instance, a marking which read 54 + DOK meant the fourth aircraft (D = 4) of K reconnaissance *Staffel* of the fourth *Geschwader* pertaining to *Luftkreis V*.

E The markings of trainer aircraft were as follows: 1st digit—o = Training Area HQ[1]; 2nd digit—1 = short-range reconnaissance aircraft; 2 = long-range reconnaissance aircraft; 3 = fighter aircraft; 4 (unassigned); 5 = bomber aircraft; 6 = dive-bomb aircraft; 7 = auxiliary aircraft and 8 = multi-purpose aircraft followed by Balken-

[1] The first digit was replaced by the letter S.

kreuz+. and then one of the range of markings extended from A01 to Z99 denoting the armed aircraft comprised within the Service Area of Training HQ. For instance, a marking which read 01+A22 meant a short-range reconnaissance aircraft representing the 22nd aircraft within the Training HQ service area.

F   Armed aircraft of replacement formations were marked as follows: 1st digit= *Luftkreis* number; letter E=air force replacement detachment; numbers 001–999 were used for the series numbering of the armed aircraft comprised in all the air force replacement detachments pertaining to one and the same *Luftkreis*. For instance, the marking 2E+025 meant the 25th aircraft of an air force replacement detachment in *Luftkreis II*.

Appendix E

Fighter Aircraft Markings
DRdL and ObdL Directive of July 2, 1936

Numbers and letters proved unsatisfactory for the marking of fighter aircraft, since they were not readily recognisable when aircraft were flying in open order and during aerial combat. Consequently, the following system was adopted: *Geschwader* were distinguished by the colour of the engine cowling and upper surface of the fuselage of each aircraft pertaining to one and the same Group. The allotted colours became traditional: red for the Richthofen Fighter *Geschwader*, brown for the Horst Wessel Fighter *Geschwader*, green for 232 Fighter *Geschwader*. Each individual aircraft in a *Staffel* (including reserve aircraft) bore a number (1–12) in white with a narrow black edging on each side of the fuselage, on the bottom of the fuselage level with the wings, and on the upper side of the wing root. The *Staffeln* pertaining to one and the same *Gruppe* were distinguished by white markings superimposed on the characteristically coloured engine cowling and fuselage end, as follows:

> 1st, 4th and 7th squadrons = no marking
> 2nd, 5th and 8th squadrons = white ring
> 3rd, 6th and 9th squadrons = round white spot

Exception: *Geschwader* displaying a light shade of distinguishing colour (e.g. yellow) had the additional (squadron) markings in black instead of white.

The *Gruppen* within one and the same *Geschwader* were distinguished by additional white markings located on the sides of the fuselage between the numerical aircraft marking and the *Balkenkreuz* in each case, as follows:

> I. Group = no additional marking
> II. Group = horizontal bar
> III. Group = horizontal wavy line

The *Gruppen* leader's aircraft bore, instead of a numerical marking, a forward pointing chevron marking, in white with a black edging.

The other two *Gruppen* Staff aircraft were marked with a smaller, and open, chevron, the third of these machines being additionally distinguished by a bar across the open end of the chevron.

In addition, *Geschwader* Staff aircraft were to have been distinguished by arrow and pointed bar markings, but this provision was dropped owing to the introduction of the Bf 109 fighter aircraft.

MARKINGS

1st *Staffel* and *I. Gruppe*—no additional marking.

2nd *Staffel* and *II. Gruppe*—straight broken line, even number.
3rd *Staffel* and *III. Gruppe*—curved and non-rectilinear additional marking.

NOTE

Jagdgeschwader 131	black★
132 Richthofen	red
134 Horst Wessel	brown
232	green
233	blue★
234	orange★

★ Where determined.

Appendix F

Military Aircraft Markings

DRdL and ObdL Directive dated July 4, 1939

The markings of all military aircraft with the exception of fighters was composed of the following elements (reading from left to right when looking at the *Balkenkreuz* marking):

(1) A unit symbol denoting a higher Staff unit, a *Geschwader*, or an independent *Gruppe*, and comprising a letter and a figure.
(2) A black *Balkenkreuz* (+).
(3) A letter distinguishing individual aircraft within a *Staffel* or Staff unit.
(4) A letter distinguishing individual aircraft pertaining to a particular *Geschwader* or independent *Gruppe*.

The letters denoting the *Staffeln* to which individual aircraft belonged were coloured, as follows:

white for the 1st *Staffel* of each *Gruppe*,
red for the 2nd *Staffel* of each *Gruppe*,
yellow for the 3rd *Staffel* of each *Gruppe*.

Within one and the same *Staffel* or Staff unit, the aircraft were sequentially distinguished by coloured letters in alphabetical order (first letter after *Balkenkreuz*).

Within the *Geschwader*, the *Staffeln* or Staff units were distinguished as follows (2nd letter after the Greek cross): *Geschwader* Staff and Staff *Staffel*[1] = Letter A; Staff *I. Gruppe*[2] = B; Staff *II. Gruppe* = C; Staff *III. Gruppe* = D; Staff *IV. Gruppe* = F; Staff *V. Gruppe* = G; 1st Squadron = H; 2nd Squadron = K; 3rd Squadron = L; 4th Squadron = M; 5th = T; 10th Squadron = U; 11th Squadron = V; 12th Squadron = W; 13th Squadron = X; 14th Squadron = Y; 15th Squadron = Z; 16th Squadron = Q; 17th Squadron = J; 18th Squadron = O; 19th Squadron = E and 20th Squadron = I.

EXAMPLES

9K + DII = 4th aircraft of 1st Squadron of *Kampfgeschwader* 51; 3M + AB = 1st aircraft of Staff unit of *I Gruppe* of *Zerstörergeschwader* 2; 1H + AA = 1st aircraft of Staff unit of *Kampfgeschwader* 26 (1st aircraft of Staff *Staffel*); A1 + MA = 13th aircraft of Staff unit of *Kampfgeschwader* 53 and 2P + BA = 2nd aircraft of Staff unit of Air Division X.

[1] Staffel = Squadron.
[2] Gruppe = Group.

Appendix G

Activation Survey of the Operational Flying Units of the *Luftwaffe*

1933

AUGUST 24, 1933 — Single-seat fighter *Geschwader 1* at Rechlin (cancelled)

OCTOBER 1, 1933 — *Reklamestaffel*[1] East Germany at Neuhausen near Königsberg i.Pr.

Reklamestaffel Central Germany at Berlin-Staaken

Reklamestaffel South Germany at Fürth near Nuremberg

Air/Sea Training *Staffel* at Warnemünde

Air Service Severa

OCTOBER 27, 1933 — *Behelfsbombergeschwader 1*[2] at Berlin (Traffic Inspectorate of the *Deutsche Lufthansa*)

1934

APRIL 1, 1934

SEPTEMBER 1, 1934

JULY 15, 1934

AUGUST 1, 1934

1935

Luftkreis[3] *I Königsberg in Prussia*
Aufklstff[4](F)	1/121	Neuhausen

Luftkreis II Berlin
Aufklstff[4](F)	1/222	Prenzlau
Jagdgeschw[5]	132	Döberitz
Kampfgeschw[6]	1, 2/252	Tutow
Behelfskampfgeschw[2] of the DLH		Berlin
Flugbereitschaft[7] of the ObdL[8]		Berlin-Staaken
Fliegerstff zbV		Berlin-Staaken
Aufklgrp of the ObdL		

Luftkreis III Dresden
Aufklstff[4](H)	1/113	Kotbus
Aufklstff[4](H)	2/114	Gotha
Aufklstff[4](F)	1/324	Grossenhain

Luftkreis IV Münster
Kampfgeschw[6]	1, 2, 3/154	Fassberg

Luftkreis V München

became integrated in *Jagdgeschw 132*

Luftkreis VI Kiel
Seeaufklstff[9]	1/116	Holtenau
Seejagdstff[9]	1/136	Kiel-Holtenau
Seefliegermehrzstff[9]	1/286	List auf Sylt

Luftdienstschleppstff[10]

NOTES

(1) Advertising or Publicity Squadron
(2) Auxiliary (interim) Bomber Geschwader No. 1 (of the DLH)
(3) Air District (LK)
(4) Reconnaissance *Staffel*
(5) Fighter *Geschwader*
(6) Bomber *Geschwader*
(7) Stand-by unit of the Air Ministry (Personal transport)
(8) *ObdL = Oberbefehlshaber der Luftwaffe* Commander-in-Chief of the *Luftwaffe* (Goering)
(9) Coastal/reconnaissance, fighter and general-purpose
(10) Air service target towing *Staffel*

MARCH 28, 1935

Luftkreis I

Aufklstff (H)	1/111	Neuhausen
Aufklstff (F)	1/121	Neuhausen

Luftkreis II

Aufklstff (F)	1/222	Prenzlau
Jagdgeschw	I./132	Döberitz
Jagdgeschw	II./132	Damm
Kampfgeschw	1, 2, 3/252	Tutow
Kampfgeschw	II./352	Greifswald
Kampfgeschw	652	Finsterwalde
Sturtzkampfgeschw	1./162	Schwerin
Behelfskampfgeschw	172	Berlin
Flugbereitschaft of the ObdL		Berlin
Aufklgrp ObdL		Berlin

Luftkreis III

Aufklstff (H)	1/113	Kottbus
Kampfgeschw	553	Merseburg
Kampfgeschw	753	Gotha

Luftkreis IV

Aufklstff (F)	1/424	Kassel
Aufklstff (H)	1/214	Münster
Aufklstff (H)	2/214	Münster
Kampfgeschw	1, 2, 3/154	Fassberg

Luftkreis V

Aufklstff (H)	1/315	Göppingen
Aufklstff (H)	2/315	Göppingen
Aufklstff (F)	1/525	Würzburg
Kampfgeschw	455	Giebelstadt

Luftkreis VI

Küstenaufklstff	1/116	Holtenau
Küaufklstff (M)	2/116	Norderney
Küaufklstff (F)	1/126	List auf Sylt
KüJagdstff	1/136	Kiel-Holtenau
KüJagdstff	2/136	Kiel-Holtenau
Seefliegermehrzstff	1/286	Kist auf Sylt
Luftdienstschleppstff		

1936/37

Luftkreis I

Stab u Aufklgr (H)	111	Neuhausen
Aufklstff (H)	1/111	Neuhausen
Aufklstff (H)	2, 3/111	Insterburg

Stab u Aufklgr (F)	121	Neuhausen	
Aufklstff (F)	1, 2, 3/121	Neuhausen	
Jagdgr	I./131	Jesau	
Jagdstff	2/131	Seerappen	

Luftkreis II

Stab u Aufklgr (H)	112	Stargard	
Aufklstff (H)	1, 2, 3/112	Stargard[1]	
Stab u Aufklgr (F)	122	Prenzlau	
Aufklstff (F)	1, 2, 3/122	Prenzlau[2]	
Stab u Aufklgr (H)	212	Kottbus	
Stab u Jagdgeschw	132	Döberitz	Richthofen
Stab u Jagdgr	I./132	Döberitz	Richthofen
Stab u Jagdgr	II./132	Damm	Richthofen
Stab u Jagdgr	I./232	Bernburg	
Stab u Kampfgeschw	152	Greifswald	Hindenburg[3, 4, 5]
Stab u Kampfgr	III./152	Barth	Hindenburg
Behelfskampfgeschw	252	Tutow	
Kampfgeschw	652	Finsterwalde[6]	
Stab u Sturzkampfgeschw	162	Schwerin	Immelmann
Sturzkampfstff	1/162	Schwerin	Immelmann[7]
Stab u Sturzkampfgr	II./162	Lübeck	Immelmann
Stab u Behelfskampfgeschw	172	Berlin	
Behelfskampfgr		Tutow	
Behelfskampfgr		Fassberg	
Streckenschule		Berlin	
Flugereitschaft of the ObdL		Berlin-Staaken	
Aufklgr of the ObdL		Berlin-Staaken	
Wettererkundungsstff			
LN Lehr- u Vers Rgt	1, 2/LN 100	Köthen[13]	

Luftkreis III

Stab u Aufklgr (F)	123	Grossenhain	
Aufklstff (F)	2/123	Grossenhain	
Stab u Kampfgeschw	153	Merseburg	
Stab u Kampfgr	III./153	Altenburg	
Stab u Kampfgeschw	253	Gotha	General Wever
Stab u Kampfgr	II./253	Erfurt	General Wever
Stab u Kampfgr	III./253	Nordhausen	General Wever

Luftkreis IV

Stab u Aufklgr (H)	114	Münster	
Aufklstff (H)	3/114	Münster	
Stab u Aufklgr (F)	124	Kassel	
Aufklstff (F)	2/124	Kassel	
Stab u Jagdgeschw	134	Dortmund	Horst Wessel
Stab u Jagdgr	I./134	Dortmund	Horst Wessel
Stab u Jagdgr	II./134	Werl	Horst Wessel
Stab u Jagdgr	III./134	Lippstadt	Horst Wessel[8]
Stab u Kampfgeschw	154	Hannover	Boelke[9]

| *Stab u Kampfgr* | II./154 | Delmenhorst | Boelke[9] |
| *Stab u Kampfgr* | I./254 | Wunstorf[10] | |

Luftkreis V

Stab u Aufklgr (H)	115	Göppingen
Stab u Aufklgr (F)	125	Würzburg
Aufklstff (F)	2, 3/125	Würzburg[1]
Stab u Jagdgr	I./135	Bad Aibling
Stab u Kampfgeschw	155	Ansbach[11]
Stab u Kampfgr	II./155	Ansbach
Stab u Kampfgr	III./155	Schwäbisch-Hall
Stab u Kampfgeschw	255	Landsberg
Stab u Kampfgeschw	355	Gablingen
Stab u Sturzkampfgr	I./165	Kitzingen[12]

Luftkreis VI (*Aufstellung until 1938*)

Küflggr	106	Nordernay
Küflggr	206	Nordernay
Küaufklstff	1/306	Nordernay
Küflggr	406	List/Sylt
Küflggr	506	West Dievenow/Wollin
Küflggr	706	Kamp
Küjagdgr	I./136	Jever
Trägerstff	I./186	Burg b Magdeburg
Bordflgstff	1/196	Wilhelmshaven
Bordflgstff	5/196	Kiel-Holtenau
Luftdienstkommando	1	Nordernay
(*Luftdienstschlepp- u*	4	Holtenau
Flugzielstaffel)	7	Wustrow

NOTES

(1) Formation of Reconnaissance Training and Experimental Squadron from 1/112 and 3/125, at Jüterbog.
(2) Pertaining to *LG 1* as from July 1, 1936.
(3) Formation of *Lehrgeschwader LG 1* at Greifswald from *II./Kampfgeschwader Hindenburg No. 152*, as from July 1, 1936.
(4) Formation of *Kampfgruppe zbV 1*, at Fürstenwalde, from *IV./Kampfgeschwader Hindenburg No. 152* (1937).
(5) Transferred to Neubrandenburg as from October 1, 1936.
(6) Becomes C-Grade Flying School.
(7) 1/*Sturzkampfgeschwader Immelmann No. 162* to *LG 1* as from July 1, 1936.
(8) *III./Jagdgeschwader Horst Wessel No. 134* divided up to form *I./JG 234* stationed at Cologne, and *II./JG 234* and *III./JG 234*, both stationed at Düsseldorf.
(9) Owing to dividing up of *LK IV* to form *LK IV* and *LK VII*.
(10) *KG 154* re-formed into *Kampfgeschwader Boelke No. 157* stationed at Hanover-Langenhagen, and *KG 254* re-formed into *KG 257* stationed at Lüneburg; parts of *KG 254* remained at Lippstadt.
(11) After the merger (*Anschluss*) of Austria with the German *Reich*, *KG 155* became *KG 158* stationed at Wiener Neustadt.

(12) Later *II./165* at Wertheim.
(13) Air Signals Detachment 100.

After *LK IV* was divided up, the following units were formed:

Luftkreis IV
Aufklgr (H) *114* at Münster.
Aufklgr (F) *124* at Kassel.
I., II., III./*JG 134 Horst Wessel* at Dortmund.
I., II./*JG 234* at Cologne and Düsseldorf.
I./*JG 334* at Wiesbaden.

Luftkreis VII
Aufklgr (F) *127* at Goslar.
I./*JG 137* at Bernburg.
I., II., III./*KG 157 Boelke* at Hannover-Langenhagen.
I., II., III./*KG 257* at Lüneburg.

LUFTWAFFE UNITS AND UNIT CODES, JULY 1, 1939

Fernaufklärer (Long-range reconnaissance units)

The four staffs of the reconnaissance-units (*Gruppen*) F 121, F 122, F 123 and F/ObdL were subordinated:

$$25 \text{ (F) } Staffeln \text{ divided into:}$$
$$20 \text{ } Staffeln \text{ Do } 17$$
$$1 \text{ } Staffel \text{ He } 111$$
$$\text{Bf } 110$$

$$
\begin{array}{ll}
3(\text{F})/10 & = \text{T}1+ \\
2, 3, 4(\text{F})/11 & = 6\text{M}+ \\
4(\text{F})/14 & = 5\text{F}+ \\
1, 2, 3(\text{F})/22 & = 4\text{N}+ \\
1, 2, 3(\text{F})/31 & = 5\text{D}+ \\
1(\text{F})/120 & = \text{A}6+ \\
1, 2, 3, 4(\text{F})/121 & = 7\text{A}+ \\
1, 2, 3(\text{F})/122 & = \text{F}6+ \\
1, 2, 3(\text{F})/123 & = 4\text{U}+ \\
1(\text{F})/124 & = \text{G}2+ \\
1, 2(\text{F})/\text{ObdL} & = \text{K}9+ \text{ also G}2+ \\
7, 8/\text{LG } 2 & = \text{L}2+ \\
\end{array}
$$

Wekusta/ObdL (Long-range weather recon.) = T5+
/LN 100 (Air Signals Detachment) = later 6N+

Nahaufklärer (Short-range reconnaissance and Army co-operation)

$$30 \text{ (H) } Staffeln \text{ divided into:}$$
$$25 \text{ } Staffeln \text{ Hs } 126$$
$$5 \text{ } Staffeln \text{ He } 45 \text{ and } 46$$

$$
\begin{array}{ll}
1, 2(\text{H})/10 & = \text{T}1+ \\
1(\text{H})/11 & = 6\text{M}+ \\
1, 2, 3, 4(\text{H})/12 & = \text{H}1+ \\
\end{array}
$$

$$1, 2, 3, 4(H)/13$$
$$1, 2, 3(H)/14 \quad =5H+$$
$$1, 2, 3, 4(H)/21 \quad =P2+$$
$$4(H)/22 \quad =4N+$$
$$4(H)/23 \quad =4E+$$
$$1, 2, 3(H)/31 \quad =5D+$$
$$1, 2, 3(H)/41 \quad =C2+$$
$$9/LG \ 2=L2+$$

Jäger (Single-seat fighter)

13 *Gruppen* divided in 39 *Staffeln*
12 *Gruppen* Bf 109
1 *Staffel*   Ar 68 (28)
I./JG 1
I./JG Richthofen No. 2
I./JG 3
I., II./JG Schlageter No. 26
I./JG 51
I./JG 52
I., II./JG 53
I./JG 76
I., II./JG 77
I. (Jagd)/LG 2
10/JG Richthofen No. 2 (Nightfighter)

attached to these were:

I./JG 20 (Nightfighter) 3 *Staffeln*
I./JG 21 (Nightfighter) 3 *Staffeln*
I., III./JG 54   6 *Staffeln*
1, 2/JG 70
1, 2/JG 71
II./JG 71 (Nightfighter) 3 *Staffeln*
10, 11 (Nachtjagd)/JG 72
11 (Nachtjagd)/LG 2

Zerstörer (Two-seat Long-range fighter, Destroyer)

9 *Gruppe* divided in 27 *Staffeln* Bf 110:
I., II./ZG 1=6U+
I./ZG 2=3M+
I., II., III./ZG Horst Wessel No. 26=U8+
I./ZG 52=A2+   (+2 *Staffeln*)
I./ZG 76=M8+
I (Zerstörer)/LG 1=L1+

(+3 *Staffeln*)

Kampfflieger (Medium-bomber)

30 *Gruppen* divided in 90 *Staffeln*
18 *Gruppen* He 111
11 *Gruppen* Do 17

1 *Gruppe* Ju   86

I./*KG Hindenburg* No. *1*=V4+
IV./*KG Hindenburg* No. *1*=*KG zbV 1*=1Z+
I., II./*KG 2*=U5+
II., III./*KG 3*=5K+
I., II., III./*KG General Wever* No. *4*=5J+
I., II./*KG 26*=1H+
I., II., III./*KG Boelke* No. *27*=1G+
II./*KG 28*=1T+
I./*KG 51*=9K+
I., II., III./*KG Legion Condor* No. *53*=A1+
I./*KG 54*=B3+
I., II./*KG 55*=G1+
I., III./*KG 76*=F1+
I., II., III./*KG 77*=3Z+

II., III. (*Kampf*)/*LG 1*=L1+
II./*LG 3*=*KG 152*=3X+

Sturzkampfflieger (Dive-bomber)

9 *Gruppen* divided in 27 *Staffeln* Ju 87

I./*StG 1*=A5+
I., II., III./*StG Immelmann* No. *2*=T6+
III./*StG 51*=6G+
I./*StG 76*=F1+
I., II./*StG 77*=S2+
II. (*Sturzkampf*)/*LG 1*=L1+

Schlachtflieger (Ground-attack)

II. (*Schlacht*)/*LG 2*=L2+

Seeflieger (Coastal)

5 *Gruppen* divided in 20 *Staffeln* (+1 *Staffel 3/186*)
1 *Staffel* Do Wal
5 *Staffeln* Do 18
5 *Staffeln* He 59
5 *Staffeln* He 60
1 *Staffel* He 115
1 *Staffel* Ar 196
1 *Staffel* Ju 87
2 *Staffeln* Bf 109

Seenahaufklärer (Short-range coastal reconnaissance)

1/*106*=M2+
1/*306*
1/*406*=K6+
1/*506*=S4+
1/*706*=6T+

Seefernaufklärer (**Maritime reconnaissance**)

$2/106 = M2+$
$2/306$
$2/406 = K6+$
$2/506 = S4+$
$2/606 = 7T+$
$10/LG\ 2 = L2+$

Küstenmehrzweckflieger (**Coastal-utility**)

$3/106 = M2+$
$3/406 = K6+$
$3/506 = S4+$
$3/706 = GT+$

Bordflieger (**Shipboard reconnaissance**)

$1/196 = 6W+$
$5/196 = 6W+$

Trägersturzkampfflieger (**Carrier-based Dive-bomber**)

$4/186$

Trägerjagdflieger (**Carrier-based single-seat fighter**)

$3/186$
$6/186$

Seenotflieger (**Air-sea rescue**)

$1/$*Seenotstaffel* D-A . . .

Appendix H

Leaders of the Fighter, Ground Attack and *Kampfgruppen* zbV

Fighter units (August 1, 1938)

I./JG 131	Jesau	Woldenga, Hptm.
Kommodore of the JG Richthofen		
No. 132	Döberitz	v Massow, Obstlt.
I./JG 132	Döberitz	Viek, Maj.
II./JG 132	Damm	Huth, Maj.
III./JG 132	Damm	Dr.-Ing. Bormann, Maj.
IV./JG 132	Werneuchen	Osterkamp, Obstlt.
Kommodore of the JG Horst Wessel		
No. 134	Dortmund	v Döring, Oberst.
I./JG 134	Dortmund	Frommherz, Obstlt.
II./JG 134	Werl	Vollbracht, Maj.
IV./JG 134	Dortmund	Schalk, Hptm.
Kommodore of the JG 234		unengaged
I./JG 234	Köln	Ritter v Schleich, Obstlt.
II./JG 234	Düsseldorf	Grabmann, Hptm.
III./JG 234	Düsseldorf	Lessmann, Hptm.
Kommodore of the JG 334	Wiesbaden	Junck, Obstlt.
I./JG 334	Wiesbaden	Witt, Maj.
II./JG 334	Mannheim	Merhart v Bernegg, Maj.
III./JG 334	Mannheim	Schmidt-Coste, Hptm.
Kommodore of the JG 135		unengaged
I./JG 135	Aibling	Ibel, Obstlt.
II./JG 135	Aibling	Stoltenhoff, Maj.
I./JG 136	Jever	Schumacher, Maj.
I./JG 137	Bernburg	Gentzen, Hptm.
II./JG 137	Zerbst	Freiherr v Houwald, Maj.
I./JG 138	Aspern	Müller, Hptm.
I./(leichte Jagd)		
Lehrgeschwader	Garz	Trübenbach, Hptm.

Ground attack groups (September 1, 1938)

Fliegergruppe 10	Tutow	Graf v Pfeil and Klein-Ellguth, Hptm.
20	Tutow	Rentsch, Maj.
30	Fassberg	v Eschwege, Hptm.
40	Fassberg	Spielvogel, Maj.
50	Lechfeld	v Kornatzki, Hptm.

Kampfgruppen zbV (**September 1, 1938**)

KG zbV	1	Fürstenwalde	Morzik, Obstlt.
	2	Briest/	
		Westhavelland	v Lindemann, Obstlt.
	3	Tutow	Leesemann, Obstlt.
	5	Fassberg	Alefeld, Obstlt.
	6	Lechfeld	Krahl, Maj.

Appendix I

Luftwaffe and RAF Rank Equivalents

Luftwaffe	*Royal Air Force*
Flieger/Funker/Kanonier	Aircraftman (2)/Signalman/Gunner
Gefreiter	Aircraftman (1)
Obergefreiter	Leading Aircraftman
Hauptgefreiter	Senior Aircraftman
Unteroffizier	Corporal
Feldwebel	Sergeant
Oberfeldwebel	Flight Sergeant
Leutnant	Pilot Officer
Oberleutnant	Flying Officer
Hauptmann	Flight Lieutenant
Major	Squadron Leader
Oberstleutnant	Wing Commander
Oberst	Group Captain
Generalmajor	Air Commodore
Generalleutnant	Air Vice Marshal
General der Flieger	Air Marshal
Generaloberst ⎫ Generalfeldmarschall ⎭	Air Chief Marshal
Reichsmarschall	Marshal of the Royal Air Force

Under the terms of the treaty of Versailles, the Germans had to reduce their army to 4,000 officers and 100,000 other ranks; their air service had to be disbanded, and its aircraft destroyed. Even prototype civil aircraft, like the E/20 designed by Adolf Rohrbach and built by the Zeppelin Werke GmbH, below, had to be dismantled

General Hans von Seeckt was Chief of the Army General Staff in the period immediately following the First World War. He did much to pave the way for the revived German air service

Hauptmann Wilberg was the air defence advisor to the Army Chief of Staff, *Luftschutzreferat im Truppenamt TA(L)*; he is pictured here later in his career, when he held the rank of General

Hauptmann Student headed the section responsible for aviation matters in the Army Office; he too rose to high rank and in this picture, taken in 1939, he is wearing the uniform of Generalmajor

Hauptmann Wimmer directed the aviation section in the Army Ordnance Office, *Herreswaffenamt HWaA*, from October 1, 1929. This picture shows him as a Generalleutnant

Generalmajor von Mittelberger, the inspector of weapon schools and the secret Air Force, 1930. He used the cover name 'Molt'

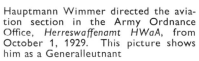

Oberstleutnant Felmy, the Chief of Staff of the inspecting branch of the secret *Luftwaffe* in May 1930

Lipezk, the secret German training airfield in Russia. Above, the permanent buildings bordering the airfield. Below, a line up of Dutch-built Fokker D XIII fighters, taken in 1927; note the lack of national markings. Fifty aircraft of this type were brought to Russia in the summer of 1925, on board the steamer *Edmund Hugo Stinnes 4*; the fighter was powered by a single 450hp Napier Lion engine which gave it a maximum speed of 160mph, and it was armed with two rifle-calibre machine guns

Above, Fokkers in the No 1 Hangar at Lipezk, and below,
six of these machines get airborne

Winter at Lipezk: a Fokker D XIII on skis

As late as the autumn of 1929, two First World War Fokker D VIIs were being used for training at Lipezk

The Heinkel HD 17 biplane served at Lipezk as a two-seater trainer, and also as a short-range reconnaissance machine. Powered by a Napier Lion engine, it had a maximum speed of 140mph and could carry a single flexible 7.9mm machine gun in the rear cockpit

The Junkers A 20, an all-round monoplane, about to start up for a night training flight from a *Deutsche Verkehrsfliegerschule*

During flying training there are always accidents. Above, a
Fokker D XIII which came to grief. Below, another Fokker
D XIII which stood on her nose; note the 'uniforms' worn by
the men

The Junkers W 33 above, and the F 13
below: aircraft of these types were used
as courier aircraft at Lipezk

The little Albatros L 69 was used as an elementary trainer, while the more powerful Heinkel HD 21 was used to teach pilots air combat tactics

Right. On December 1, 1922, Ernst Heinkel opened his aircraft factory beside the airfield at Warnemünde

A secret visit to Warnemünde by *Reichswehr* officers wearing civilian clothes: from left to right, Kapitaen Luebecke, the commander of the Swedish Air Force, Ernst Heinkel, Hauptmann Student (later commanded the German Paratroop Army), Karl Schwaerzler, Hauptmann Baeumker, Leutnant Johannesson, Leutnant (retired) Reinau, Oberleutnant Jeschonnek (his brother later became Chief of the Air Staff), and test-pilot Weichel

During the Ruhr crisis in 1923, the German Navy bought ten Heinkel
He 1 seaplane fighters. The aircraft were assembled and tested in
Sweden, then dismantled and stored in crates in Stockholm. In the
photograph below, the aircraft are seen flying in Swedish markings

In 1926 the German Navy held a seaplane competition at
Warnemünde, offering a prize of 360,000 Marks (about
£32,800) to the winner. The first prize went to the Heinkel
He 5a above, and below this three seater was powered by a
450 horsepower Napier Lion engine and flown by Wolfgang
V. Gronau

Second and third in the seaplane competition, respectively,
were the Junkers W 33 above, and the Heinkel HD 24 below

The German Army watched the seaplane competition with great interest. Here
von Richthofen (left, with his back to the camera) is pictured with Professor
Junkers (right, with his back to the camera)

The Roland Ro VII *Robbe* (seal), a twin-engined flying boat, it was not successful in the competition

When it first flew, in 1927, the twelve-engined Dornier X was the largest heavier-than-air machine to fly. Although the flying boat was referred to as a passenger carrier, the project was in fact financed by the German Navy, who were interested in a very long-range reconnaissance and mine and torpedo carrying aircraft

Types built by Heinkel for the German Navy, to keep abreast of the state-of-the-art: above, the He 9, a general purpose seaplane, and below the He 22 a trainer

The Heinkel He 42, trainer seaplane

The Navy used the four-seater long-range Heinkel 10 for
propagation trials with its latest radio equipment

In order to enable seaplanes to undergo combat-testing at Lipezk, which lay deep in Russia far from the sea, some machines were fitted with wheeled undercarriages instead of their floats. Types thus modified were the Heinkel 38, see left above on wheels, and left below on floats, and the Heinkel 59 above and below

The Heinkel HD 41, built in 1929 to Army specifications, was designed to fill the roles of long-range reconnaissance machine and also medium bomber

Throughout the German tenure of the training base at Lipezk, the Russians followed closely German developments in aviation. In this photograph, from Ernst Heinkel's guest book, Russian visitors are pictured in front of an He 38 fighter at the Heinkel works. There are no prizes for picking out the Russians!

The Arado 64 fighter, powered by a 450 horsepower Siemens radial, was developed in 1929 to Army specifications and tested at Lipezk

Among the types tested at Lipezk during 1930–31 were the Heinkel 45 reconnaissance-bomber, above, and the Arado 65 fighter below; the latter type was later widely used by the so-called 'Advertising Squadrons'

The first prototype of the Heinkel 46
was a biplane, above. But while it was
still in the flight trials stage the lower
wing was removed, and the type entered
service as a parasol-winged monoplane,
below

The Junkers K 47 two-seat interceptor fighter was interesting in that it was a
monoplane of all metal construction—two advanced features for a machine that
appeared in 1929. However this aircraft, which was built in Sweden for the
clandestine German Air Service, proved inferior to conventional biplanes during
comparative trials at Lipezk

The simple bomb rack which could be fitted to the K 47s undercarriage

Three heavy bombers which were tested at Lipezk: the Dornier 'P', the Rohrbach Roland and the Dornier 11. The Dornier 'P' left above, carried a crew of six, and was powered by four Bristol Jupiter engines in unusal tandem mountings. The Dornier 11, left below, which was later placed into production, featured a retractable undercarriage. The unusual Rohrbach Roland above and below, was a three-engined aircraft, with gun positions built into the engine nacelles as well as the rear fuselage

Two small primary trainers: The Udet 12 'Flamingo' above, and the BFW-1 *Sperber* ('Sparrowhawk') below. The latter type was one of the early designs of Willy Messerschmitt

After Adolf Hitler was elected to power he used as his personal transport a Junkers 52, numbered D-2600 and later named *Immelmann* after the First World War flying ace

Left, Heinkel 51 fighters of the secret German Air Service,
wearing civil markings, over Germany. Above, the new
German Air Minister, Hermann Goering, inspects men of the
secret Air Service at Schleissheim near Munich in 1934;
in the row nearest the camera are officer cadets Falk, Radusch
and Trautloft, all of whom were to reach senior rank during
the war

The *Luftwaffe* comes into the open. On March 14, 1935, during a parade held in public at Berlin/Doeberitz, Hitler accepts 'Advertising Squadron Central Germany', *DVL— Reklame Staffel Mitteldeutchland*, into the new Air Force as *I/Gruppe of Jagdgeschwader* 132 *Richthofen*

Right, on his 46th birthday, April 20, 1935, Hitler received *I/Gruppe of JG* 134 *Horst Wesel* into the *Luftwaffe*. Like I/JG 132, this unit was equipped with the Heinkel 51

Hitler being shown over the cockpit of a Heinkel 45

Junkers 52 bombers of *Kampfgeschwader* 154, pictured at Fassberg in 1935. Of interest is the *Reichskriegsflagge* (Reich War Flag), which still bears the iron cross; on November 7 of that year the flag was replaced by a new one bearing the swastika

During the large parade held at Gatow airfield near Berlin, on April 21, 1936, Goering handed over new standards to several *Luftwaffe* units

To encourage a high degree of air mindedness in the youth of Germany, the Nazi party sponsored model aircraft flying and glider competitions, many of them with valuable prizes. Below, members of the Hitler Youth prepare a Schneider SG 38 primary glider for launching, at the school at Moringen, near Nordheim

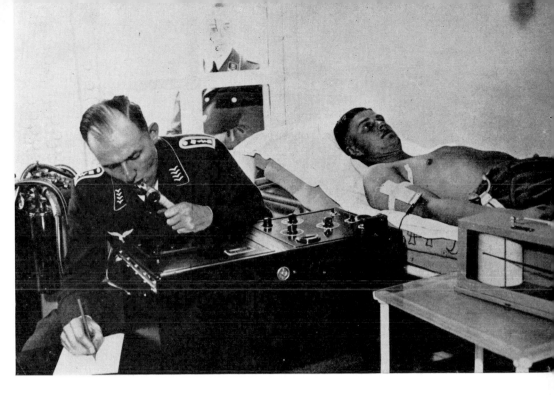

Places in the new *Luftwaffe* were eagerly sought after, and entry standards were high. Here recruits undergo a comprehensive medical examination

Above, taking the oath of allegiance

The same in any armed service anywhere: left above, recruits leaving the stores with their newly issued kit; left below, the interminable 'square bashing'

Student pilots parading in front of their aircraft, before flying

Primary training aircraft used by the *Luftwaffe*: below, the Focke Wulf 44 *Stieglitz* (Goldfinch)

Above, the Heinkel 72

Below, the Klemm 35B

Left, advance training types: the Focke Wulf 56, the Gotha 145 and the Arado 76

Above and below, specialised trainers: the Junkers W 33, for instrument flying training, and the Focke Wulf 58, for twin-engined training

The hangar at an A/B training school, packed with aircraft. Among the types that can be recognised are the Fw 44 and the Go 145

An air force flies on the sweat of its groundcrews, and much depends upon the quality of their training. Above, engine mechanics learn about the diesel engine fitted to the Junkers 86.

Above, pupils learn about the blind-flying instrument panel; either this shot was 'set up' by the photographer, or else the instructor was demonstrating a very bad lecture technique—the men at the back can have no idea what he was pointing out

The annually-held *Reichsparteitag* (Reich Party Day), at Nuremberg, was the most impressive military spectacle held in Germany during the 1930s. Left, Junkers 52 bombers pass over the drawn-up ranks of soldiers. Above, the formations fly across the city of Nuremberg, below, the arena seen from the air, with the shadows of the bombers

Preparing for the day's flying. A mechanic checks the
BMW VI water-cooled motor of a Heinkel 51

Fighter pilots receive their pre-flight briefing

Above, ground handling of an He 51; the elaborate steering dolly is interesting. Below, a line-up of He 51 As of *JG 132*

Right above, an He 51 prepares for take-off; note the Gruppe commander's insignia immediately behind the motor. Right below, two He 51s engage in a mock dog-fight

Heinkel 51s. Left above, a *Rotte* (pair) of these aircraft take-off; note that the wheel spats have been removed for rough-field operations. Left below, a *Staffel* formation

In the late summer of 1936 the first Arado 68 fighters entered service in the *Luftwaffe* to replace some of the He 51s; the new fighter was powered by a Jumo 210, and like the He 51 it was armed with two 7.9mm machine guns. Above, groundcrew prepare Ar 68s for take-off. Below, air to ground gunnery practice in an Ar 68

In 1934 the German Air Ministry invited tenders for a more modern design to replace the He 51 and Ar 68 fighters. Four new types were produced to meet the specification: the Arado 80, above, and the Focke Wulf 159 below

The Heinkel 112 and the Messerschmitt
109 above and below. Following flight
trials, the Messerschmitt 109 was chosen
as the standard single-engined fighter for
the *Luftwaffe*

Above, a line-up of Bf 109 B fighters. This version was the first production model of this aircraft, and was issued to *Jagdgeschwader* 132 in 1937. Below, pilots of *JG* 132 in a practice scramble at Doeberitz airfield. Right, a close-up of the Jumo motor installation in the Bf 109 B. Note the firing port for the MG 17 machine gun which fired through the airscrew hub, two further machine guns were mounted on top of the engine, and were synchronised to fire through the airscrew disc

The Dornier 23 bomber was a development of the earlier Do 11 and Do 13 aircraft, but featured the retrograde step of a fixed undercarriage in place of the troublesome retractable undercarriage fitted to its predecessors. The type was issued in fairly large numbers to the newly-forming bomber units. Below, Do 23s of *KG* 153 on their way to Nuremberg for the Armed Forces Day fly-past in September 1936. Right, the gun positions in the Do 23: above, the mid upper gunner with his 7.9mm machine gun; below, the ventral gunner

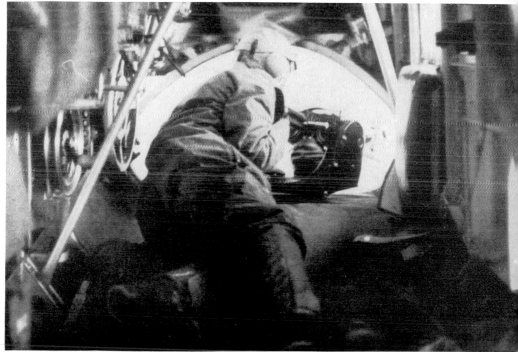

Originally designed as an airliner, the Junkers 52 was employed as a bomber by some *Luftwaffe* units. The military version was armed with two machine guns, and could carry six 550lb bombs, or 24 110lb, or 96 22lb bombs. Above, Ju 52s of *KG* 152, showing the mid-upper and ventral gun positions. Below, Ju 52s in Vee formation

Observers training with a bomb sight simulator

The Junkers 86 replaced the Ju 52 and the Do 23 in some bomber units, but it was soon relegated to second-line tasks, because with its two diesel motors the performance was only mediocre. Left above, a Ju 86 of KG 253; note the splinter camouflage on the upper surfaces of the wings. Left below, Ju 86s in formation. Above, the nose gun and bomb aiming position of the Ju 86; below, the rotatable semi-retractable ventral gun turret

The Heinkel 111 entered service in the late autumn of 1936. The first unit to receive it was *Kampfgeschwader* 154 *Boelke*, at Hannover-Langenhagen. Below, a close-up showing the open mid-upper gun position and retractable ventral 'dustbin' fitted to early versions. Right above, the '71' in front of the fuselage cross identifies this He 111 as belonging to *KG*154; the style of the number '1' is unusual. Below, groundcrewmen prepare to load a 550lb bomb into an He 111; in this aircraft the bombs were suspended in the bomb-bay by their noses, and the nose suspension ring can be clearly seen

The Dornier 17 was initially produced to meet a Lufthansa requirement for a high speed mail carrier, but became an extremely successful high-speed bomber and reconnaissance aircraft. The early bomber versions were armed with two 7.9mm machine guns, and could carry 1,100lb of bombs. Above, a fine shot of Do 17s of KG 155, one of the first units to receive the type. Below, a Do 17 E of KG 255; note the black disc marking, painted on for manoeuvres in 1937

Right, Dornier 17 at night

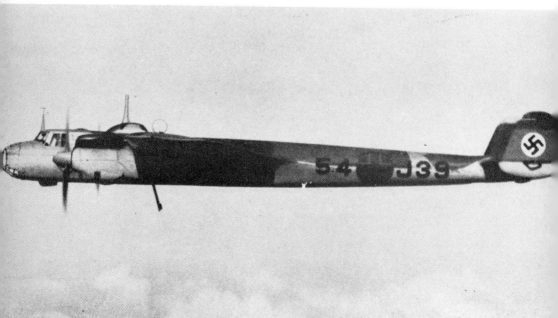

Do 17s on exercise

To meet a *Luftwaffe* requirement to equip a long-range strategic bomber arm, the German industry produced prototypes of the Dornier 19 and the Junkers 89. But both machines were hopelessly underpowered, and their performance was so poor that they were cancelled in 1937 in favour of the more advanced Heinkel 177. Above and below, the Do 19, powered by four 650 horsepower Bramo 322 motors. Right, the Junkers 89; in the background of the photograph below, taken at Dessau in the winter of 1936, is the first prototype of the Junkers 88

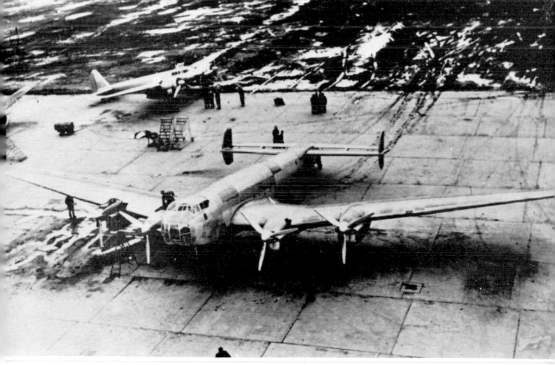

Destined to become the most successful bomber and general purpose type in the wartime *Luftwaffe*, the Junkers 88 grew out of a German Air Ministry requirement for a fast medium bomber, issued in the spring of 1935. Unsuccessful competing types were the Henschel 124 and the Focke Wulf 57. The Ju 88 entered service with the trials unit *Erprobungskommando* 88 in the spring of 1939; at that time it was the fastest medium bomber in the world, with a top speed of 280mph

Seen with Goering, Colonel Ernst Udet, who was the top-scoring German First World War fighter pilot to survive the conflict. Appointed to head the *Luftwaffe* Technical Office, Udet received from Goering two Curtiss F11 C 'Hawk' aircraft for his own personal use, below, Udet flew them during air displays, and also in dive-bombing trials

The initial equipment of the *Luftwaffe* dive-bomber units, the Heinkel 50 above, and the Arado 65 below, did not remain long in first line service. The He 50 had originally been developed as a dive-bomber for the Japanese Navy, but was never delivered to that service

The Henschel 123 replaced the He 50 and the Ar 65 in the dive-bomber units.
A strongly-built biplane, it was powered by a 580 horsepower BMW 132 motor
and could carry a bomb load of one 550lb and four 110lb bombs

Above, the two forward firing 7.9mm guns of an Hs 123 being harmonised with the gunsight at the firing butts. Below, crews receive their final briefing from the *Staffelkapitaen* prior to a flight

Above, an Hs 123 of 2/StG 162 *Immelmann* taxies out for take-off. Below, a *Kette* formation of three of these aircraft

It was with the Junkers 87 that the *Luftwaffe Stuka* (Stuka is a contraction of *Sturzkampfflugzeug*, meaning 'dive-bomber') units were to carve their place in history. The Ju 87A entered service with *I/StG* 162 *Immelmann* in the spring of 1937. Powered by a 680 horsepower Jumo 210 motor, it carried a single 550lb bomb under the fuselage

Moving bombs from the dump to the waiting dive-bombers

Armourers loading a 550lb bomb to a Ju 87A. The crutch, designed to push the bomb out and clear of the airscrew when the aircraft was in a steep dive, may be seen resting on the bomb. Note also the engine starter handle, sticking down from the engine cowling

A *Staffel* of Junkers 87 As

The *Luftwaffe* was built up as an arm to support the German Army, and aerial reconnaissance was rightly regarded as being of vital importance. The crew of a Heinkel 46 receive last minute instructions prior to a flight

An observer with the hand-operated Zeiss C/5a camera

The Heinkel 45 equipped the first long-range reconnaissance units

The Heinkel 45

The Heinkel 46, the first tactical reconnaissance aircraft issued to the new *Luftwaffe*. Note the position of the observer during photography in the picture below

The information on reconnaissance photographs can become out-dated very rapidly, so it is important that films be processed quickly. Above, a mobile dark room, below, removing the film for developing

The next stage in the reconnaissance process, and one demanding great skill: photographic interpretation

The Henschel 126, which flew for the first time in 1936,
replaced the He 46 in tactical reconnaissance units

The Heinkel 70 *Blitz* (Lightning) was built as a high-speed commercial aircraft for Lufthansa, but a few were used by the *Luftwaffe* in the high-speed reconnaissance role. Right, pre-flight briefing of an He 70 crew

By 1939, all *Luftwaffe* long-range reconnaissance units were equipped with the Dornier 17

During the early 1930s, the German Navy obtained a few Dornier 16 *Wal* flying boats. Above, one of these aircraft being lowered into the water prior to a flight. Below, a close-up of the unusual double gun position on the rear fuselage; both weapons are 7.9mm MG 15 machine guns

A line-up of aircraft at the seaplane station at Hoernum in 1937. To the left, He 59 torpedo bombers of 3/*KüFlGr* 106; to the right, He 60 reconnaissance seaplanes of 1/*KüFlGr* 506

The Heinkel 51B was used in small numbers by seaplane fighter units. Left above, an aircraft of Coastal Fighter Gruppe (*Kuestenjagdgruppe*) 136 taking-off. Left below, an He 51B at the firing butts for gun and sight harmonisation

An interesting in-flight photograph of the Heinkel 59, one of the very few to show this machine carrying a torpedo

The Heinkel 60 reconnaissance float-plane was the main type to be operated from ships of the German Navy prior to the war. Right above, one of these aircraft on the catapult of the heavy cruiser *Admiral Scheer*. Right below, one of these aircraft taking off from the water

The Heinkel 114 was designed as a replacement for the He 60, but was not very successful and went into service in only very small numbers. Above, a *Kette* of these aircraft, of *Kuestenfliegergruppe* 506 getting airborne. Below, a low level 'beat up'; note the sesquiplane (one and a half wing) arrangement

The Dornier 18 long-range reconnaissance flying boat
entered service in 1938, to replace the earlier Do 16. It was
powered by two Junkers Jumo 205C diesel motors

A Junkers W 34 floatplane, employed for target towing and
communications work

The Heinkel 115 entered service in 1938, to replace the He 59 in the torpedo and general purpose seaplane role. This twin-engined floatplane had exceptionally good water handling qualities, and was to remain in service through almost the whole of the war. Below, an He 115 carries out an attack with a practice torpedo against a freighter

Following its replacement in front line units by the He 115, the He 59 saw service as an air-sea rescue floatplane. Above, one of these aircraft in flight over the Baltic coast. Below, an He 59 runs in to pick up a crew from their rubber dinghy, during an exercise

The *Luftwaffe* placed a heavy reliance on its Flak (Flak is a contraction of the word *Flieger-abwehrkanonen*, meaning 'anti-aircraft guns') arm for the defence of targets. The 88mm Flak 36 was the mainstay of the heavy Flak units; above, one of these weapons under tow, below, in the firing position. The Flak 36 was effective up to an altitude of 25,000ft, and had a rate of fire of between 15 and 20 rounds per minute

Against any but the slowest targets, heavy anti-aircraft fire is possible only with the help of a predictor device; this one is the *Kommandogeraet* 36. The heart of the device was an analogue computer, fed with information on the targets position and rate of change from the range-finder mounted along the top. The predictor calculated the azimuth and elevation for the gun, and also fed a range to enable the clockwork time-fused shells to be set correctly

During the 1930s all the major powers employed sound locators for the location of aircraft at night. But when war came it soon became clear that the device was of little use for gunlaying against aircraft flying higher than 15,000ft or faster than 180mph

Right, war does not stop when it rains, and neither do exercises. Here a crew man their 150cm searchlight during a heavy shower

During the late 1930s the *Luftwaffe* experimented with both barrage balloons and barrage kites to defend targets. The kites, above, were effective up to 15,000ft, but could not be used in winds below 12mph. The balloons, below and right, reached up to 10,000ft and could not be used if the wind speed exceeded 25mph

The most used German light Flak weapon prior to the war was the 20mm Flak 30, here seen in the firing position. In both pictures the rearmost man is seen with the small optic range finder; he was the 'Gunner No 5', and his task was to act as 'human predictor'

The *Luftwaffe* was intended for highly mobile operations, and for these good communications are vital. Above, a mobile wireless station operating under camouflage, and below, a mobile telephone exchange

Airborne wireless operator training on board a Ju 52 flying classroom. Left, taking a radio bearing: the student with his back to the camera on the left is rotating the loop aerial for a null signal. Above, students learn to plot radio bearings, to get a 'fix'

Wireless operators receiving training in morse

Senior *Luftwaffe* commanders: Generalmajor Walter Wever, the first Chief of Staff; General der Flieger Albert Kesselring, Wever's successor and later the commander of *Luftflotte 1*

Generalmajor Hans Jeschonnek was Chief of the Air Staff when war broke out. Generalleutnant Ritter von Greim was the commander of *Fliegerdivision 5* in 1939

The Spanish Civil War gave the new *Luftwaffe* its first baptism of fire. The force began by ferrying some 15,000 Moorish troops loyal to the Nationalist cause from Tetuan in Morocco to Jerez de la Frontera near Seville; at the time it was the largest military airlift ever attempted. Left, Oberst von Scheele was the commander of the first 86 German volunteers to be shipped to Spain, along with six He 51 fighters and 20 anti-aircraft guns, for the protection and support of the airlift

Initially, the Heinkel 51, above, used as a fighter over Spain, but it soon became clear that the type was outclassed by the Russian types used by the Republicans. It later served with some success as a ground attack aircraft, carrying six 20lb fragment-ation bombs. The He 51 was replaced in the fighter role by the Messerschmitt 109B-2, below, which seized and held air superiority for the Nationalists

Left, Heinkel 111B-1 bombers of *Kampfgruppe K/88* of the Legion Kondor, lined up at Avila airfield; above, aircraft of this unit take off in formation for an attack; below, in action over Catalonia—note the 'dustbin' ventral gun position

A rare picture showing a Dornier 17E of *K/88* attacking a Republican target

A Junkers 87A dive-bomber in flight over Spain. Three of
these machines were employed to test the feasibility of dive-
bombers under operational conditions

Following the success of the Ju 87A-1 trials, these were
replaced by the later Ju 87B-1. Below, a *Kette* of Ju 87B-1s
on their way to attack a target in Spain

The return of the victorious Legion Kondor. Above, Goering in person greets General-major von Richthofen (a cousin of the First World War fighter ace, and last commander of the *Luftwaffe* units in Spain) as he comes ashore at Hamburg, still in his Spanish uniform. Behind von Richthofen stands Oberst von Scheele. Below, Hitler reviews the men of the Legion Kondor in Berlin

During the final years of peace, the Reichs Party Rallies at Nuremberg became blatant exhibitions of military might. Above, Flak units parade. Right, Do 17s trail smoke as they run over the stadium in mock attack

On the diplomatic front, Hitler lost no opportunity to ensure that the strength of the new *Luftwaffe* was seen by those who mattered. Above, Air Vice Marshal E. L. Courntney visits the *Luftwaffe* academy at Berlin-Gatow in January 1937. Below, General Vuillemin, the Commander-in-Chief of the French Air Force, inspecting the *Jagdgeschwader Richthofen* at Berlin-Doeberitz in August 1938; next to Vuillemin walks Generaloberst Erhard Milch

The famous American pilot Colonel Charles Lindbergh was well received when he visited Germany, and was much impressed by what he saw. In the photograph above he is seen at the Messerschmitt works at Augsburg. From left to right: Lindbergh, Willy Messerschmitt, test pilot Fritz Wendel, Frau Strohmeier (who later became Frau Messerschmitt), test pilot Dr Wurster and the famous aerobatic pilot Stoer

In keeping with the general aim of gaining the greatest possible publicity for German aviation, the industry was encouraged to send aircraft to air shows abroad. During the International Military Aircraft Competition held at Dueben-dorf near Zurich in 1937, the Bf 109 V 13, above, won the Alpine speed circuit, and climb and dive competitions. During the same meeting the Do 17 M V1, below, won the speed circuit for multi-seater aircraft; this machine was specially up-engined for the occasion, and with its top speed of 265mph it was faster than the single-seat French Dewoitine 510 fighter

After gaining the World Air Speed Record with the Heinkel He 110 V8 on March 30, 1939, on the Heinkel company's airfield at Orianburg near Berlin. Köhler is embracing the record-breaking pilot Dieterle; on the right stands technical assistant Meschkat

Five world speed record holders, pictured in Berlin shortly before the war. From left to right: Dr Wurster, Bf 109 V13, 380mph on November 11, 1937. Fritz Wendel, Me 209 V1, 480mph on April 26, 1939. Francesco Agello, MC 72, 441mph on October 23, 1934. Ernst Udet, He 100 V2, 395mph on June 5, 1938. Hans Dieterle, He 100 V8, 465mph on March 30, 1939

On March 12, 1938, Hitler annexed Austria and the small Austrian Air Force was incorporated into the *Luftwaffe*. Above, Goering returns the salute of assembled Austrian officers. Below, Goering takes the review of an assembled Luftwaffen unit in Austria

Above, an Austrian Fiat CR 32 fighter in *Luftwaffe* markings, shortly after the annexation. Below, Austrian Fiats flying in an air display held at Vienna-Neustadt shortly after the take-over

On December 8, 1938, at a ceremony attended by Hitler, the aircraft carrier *Graf Zeppelin* was launched at the Deutsche Werke at Kiel. This vessel, intended to carry Bf 109 fighters, Ju 87 dive-bombers and Fieseler 167 torpedo and reconnaissance aircraft, was never completed; captured by Soviet forces at the end of the war, she finally sank while being towed back to Russia

Prior to the Second World War the German airborne forces, an integral part of the *Luftwaffe*, were the best equipped and trained in the world. Above, the DFS 230 transport glider; fitted with a jettisonable undercarriage for take-off and a skid for landing; it could carry a pilot and nine fully equipped assault troops. Below, paratroops board a Ju 52. Right, troopers stream out of their aircraft during an exercise

Above, Focke Wulf 200 V3, Hitler's personal aircraft immediately before the war. He did change the type of aircraft but not the registered number.

The shape of things to come. On August 27, 1939, the Heinkel 178, below, became the first aircraft in the world to fly on the power of a turbojet engine. Right, the Heinkel-Hirth centrifugal turbojet engine, which powered the He 178

New types. During the final days of peace, work was well advanced on the prototype of the new German heavy bomber, the Heinkel 177, above, in spite of its twin-engined appearance, the He 177 had four engines, with two engines driving each airscrew through a gearbox. The type made its first flight on November 19, 1939. Below, the Blohm und Voss 138 flying boat, which first flew in its production form in February 1939

By September 1939 the Heinkel 111 made up the backbone of the German heavy bomber force. The main version was the He 111, above, which featured a streamlined nose section instead of the stepped nose section of earlier types. Below, an He 111 on the compass swinging base at the maker's airfield. Right, He 111s in the final stages of assembly

At a combat airfield on the eve of hostilities. At this time the *Luftwaffe* single-engined fighter units were equipped almost entirely with the Messerschmitt 109. The E version, that in greatest use, carried an armament of two 7.9mm MG 17 machine guns synchronised to fire through the propellor disc and two wing-mounted 20mm MGFF cannon

Ready for war: above, Messerschmitt 110 heavy
fighters in formation. Below, He 111 heavy
bombers

Above, Henschel 126 battlefield reconnaissance
aircraft. Below, a Dornier 18 long-range oversea
reconnaissance flying boat

War! Above, Junkers 87 dive-bombers take off
on the morning of September 1, 1939, for targets
in Poland. Below, in flight

The first bombs fall, in a war that is to last for nearly six years, and which will end with the *Luftwaffe* smashed to pieces